Getting My First Hug

GETTING MY FIRST HUG

A FATHER'S STORY OF HIS SON'S TRIUMPH OVER AUTISM

STEVEN E. YATES

© 2013 Steven Elton Yates
Published by Kingston House Publishing

All rights reserved. No part of this publication may be reproduced, stored in a retrieval system or transmitted, in any form, or by any means, electronic, mechanical, recorded, photocopied, or otherwise, without the prior written permission of both the copyright owner and the above publisher of this book, except by a reviewer who may quote brief passages in a review.

The scanning, uploading, and distribution of this book via the Internet or via any other means without the permission of the publisher is illegal and punishable by law. Please purchase only authorized electronic editions and do not participate in or encourage electronic piracy of copyrightable materials. Your support of the author's rights is appreciated.

Designed by Vince Pannullo
Printed in the United States of America by RJ Communications.
ISBN:978-0-578-13268-6

Contents

Chapter 1: Seeing the Miracle... 13
Chapter 2: What Do We Have Here?.. 23
Chapter 3: There's Nothing Wrong With This Kid................ 53
Chapter 4: The Way Forward 61
Chapter 5: Education and Expectation 67
Chapter 6: Speaking of Sports... 75
Chapter 7: Always Bring a Gun to a Knife-fight..................... 85
Chapter 8: If At First You Don't Succeed 91
Chapter 9: Bullies - Big and Small and a Sign........................... 97
Chapter 10: Social Groups and the Transition Academy..... 111

Final Thoughts 117

Dedication

THIS collection of stories is dedicated to the most amazing person I have ever met. I can only imagine how hard he has worked to overcome the challenges that life has presented to him. I cannot admire anyone else as much as I admire him. My wife, his mother, runs a very close second. Such deep love and tenacious refusal to fail is awesome in the truest sense of the word. I once told our daughter, his sister, that he was very special and would need a very special sister and she has more than lived up to that. To the good teachers, therapists and kids who showed him kindnesses that I never saw, this is for you too. Thank you.

This work is also dedicated to my father who never panicked and could, through patience and diligent effort, work through any problem. And my father-in-law who could, through guile and gall, work his way around any problem.

This work was divinely inspired as a help, a hope and an inspiration to anyone who loves a person with special needs. Miracles can happen. Hard work, persistence and prayer are powerful tools. Remember that there will always be time to give up later, so don't do it now.

Introduction

The Road Not Taken or You Never Know

FREQUENTLY, the thought occurs to me, "What if we had done things differently? Would things be better or worse or the same if we had or hadn't taken this action or that?" And the profound truth is that we will never know. We can never know. I may feel that certain actions were unquestionably errors. And I may equally feel that certain decisions were unquestionably the right ones. But experience has taught me that there are very few straight lines between cause and effect. The best laid schemes don't always work out. And some days it is better to be lucky than good. So we'll just never know.

I often ask myself how much better of a father I could have been to my two wonderful kids as they grew up. In the earliest days of my son's life, I was in turns involved, distracted, preoccupied and consumed. How much different would things be now, if I could have been that steady, consistent bulwark of fatherly advice and action every day of his life? I will never know. We took the path we took. It got us here and there is no going back, no do-over.

As a father, I look at my kids and in them is my every lofty hope and dream. I want to see them succeed more than I ever wanted to succeed myself. Knowing my own flaws, having spent hours dwelling on them, I want to make sure they have none of them. But maybe that just means they will have other flaws. What does the ideal father do? Where does guidance end and allowing them free will begin? And how will I ever know what kind of job I did? Maybe I never will.

This is a collection of stories about my son, our son, actually, my wife's and mine. I'm going to changes all of the names but one in telling these stories. Although many of the stories involve my wife and my daughter and they are heroines of many of them, I will try to keep the focus on my son and his rise. I would like to keep me out of the story, but I just don't know how to do that. So I will try to tell my son's story through my eyes. Maybe someday he will write his own story. I hope so.

Every child is different. Our son's case is totally unique, just like all the rest. I am not an autism expert. I'm just a father who loves his son. We've seen lots of kids who have strengths and weaknesses in every area. Some do better than others. Some make progress more quickly or more slowly. Some have conditions, complications and difficulties we never had to deal with. Our hearts go out to every child with special needs and all the people who love and care for them. That's really every child.

I am not a doctor and nothing in these stories should be taken as medical advice by anyone. Nor am I a lawyer and not a word of this is legal advice. Doctors and lawyers and teachers figure in these stories. Exactly how much of a difference any of them made in the story is hard to measure. I can only try to convey my beliefs, impressions and experiences. It is my sincere hope that someone will read these stories and come away with a sense of hope for a young person in their life. But will these stories make a difference in their life? I guess I'll never really know.

But here goes.

1

Seeing the Miracle

IN the great movie, *The Ten Commandments*, the best parts are the miracles. Moses' staff turning into a snake. The burning bush. And, of course, the show-stopper, the parting of the Red Sea. In the very funny movie, *Oh, God*, God, played by George Burns, calls those kinds of miracles "special effects" and says that his last miracle was the '69 Mets.

Most of us think of miracles like that. They are rare occurrences that happened long ago. But what if miracles happen all around each of us every day? What if seeing the miracle was the rare part?

A miracle is defined as a perceptible interruption in the workings of the laws of nature, a statistically unlikely but beneficial event and sometimes, an event brought about by divine intervention.

I began to understand what a miracle is nearly twenty years ago. On a rainy May evening, I held our son for the first time. Our three year old daughter had a little brother and we had the perfect family: one of each. As we counted his ten fingers and toes that wave of relief swept over us as I imagine it does for every new parent. No one likes to talk about it, but I think there is always a fear that some part of the developmental process may go awry. That's the first of many fears that parents wade through. Later fears include the child driving, dating and choosing a mate that doesn't have a mohawk.

For the first two years, our new son was a pretty typical baby. He ate and slept a lot, cried a bit and grew. I remember my parents coming to visit and my dad remarked about his "hearty laugh". He was a happy baby and my wife doted on him as she had our daughter. She showered our children with loving attention. She sang songs to them, read stories, and played with them. There was an almost non-stop barrage of language from her to them. Our daughter was precocious and began to babble, then talk early on. Before long she was recognizing letters, making up stories and chattering non-stop in the sweetest, most adorable way possible. Given the same motherly love and treatment, I took it as given that our son would follow suit.

Of course, I was off working. Even if part of me thought I was doing something important by bringing home a paycheck, the rest of me knew my wife was really doing the important work. We all watched endless Sesame Street and Thomas the Tank Engine episodes, we had a large well-watched library of child-friendly educational videos for all seasons. We played together inside when it was cold and outside, on the swings when it was warm. Both kids loved to play in the sprinkler. And bath-time was playtime too.

It was when our son was about two that my wife mentioned to me quietly that she thought his speech was not developing on schedule. She tracked each child's development in diaries and compared the milestones to the parenting books' benchmarks of what was normal or typical. I brushed her concerns aside but a very small seed was planted in a corner of my mind that took me back to the day we had counted ten fingers and toes with such relief.

I was not equipped to understand what delayed language development was, much less how best to deal with it. So I continued to go to work figuring that time would solve whatever problems existed.

A few weeks later, she expressed her concern to me again about our son's lack of language skills. We decided to take him to the pediatrician. Surely, a doctor would know what to do.

One physical examination later, we found ourselves talking to the doctor. He largely dismissed our concerns. After all, the child was making his wants known by pointing and making noises, even if he only used a few words like "mama" and "again". He seemed to understand us when we attended to him. Boys generally talk later than girls. This is the first truism that I hung my hopes on. It's funny how I knew, even as I tried to believe it, that this was not the whole story.

Digression. - It seems impossible today, when we live in an age of information overload, that there was ever a time, in the days before the Internet, when information was hard to come by. The public library was just about the only place to go to try to find answers. And for something like juvenile speech delay, the answer might just be a reference to a newsletter or two. But my wife began to tenaciously pursue answers. I began to see these newsletters on her nightstand. She had sent off for them. Some were helpful. Some were not. She would tell me that there were other families who had kids, sons mostly, who were late talkers. She was learning about the complexities of the development of language skills in young children. I tried not to think of our son as having any such problems, but as she learned more and would share bits and pieces of what she had learned with me, I began to see that his issues might not be unique.

But one thing finally broke through my wall of denial. Both our children were loving and happy. But one day it struck me that although I had hugged and kissed our son many times, he had never hugged or kissed me. He had hugged my wife and kissed her back. There was a real connection there. And he would play with me and laugh with me, but I had never gotten one of his big, special hugs around the neck. And at that moment, that was what I suddenly wanted more than anything I had ever wanted before. I was on board. - End of digression.

A month or two later we were back at the pediatrician and had our son's hearing tested. It was fine. My wife had assembled a sheaf of newsletters from various groups. She had sorted them out and had begun to assess what our son did and did not do. These were the symptoms. But they were not symptoms that a typical pediatrician of the mid-1990s had been trained to treat. It is a hollow feeling to have your trusted doctor tell you that he can't help you with a problem your child has. If not you, doc, then who?

My wife told him about the information she had gathered. There were people who were trying various therapies from diets to massages to dangerous-sounding, pseudo-medical treatments. Might one of these help our son? The doctor said he would not perform any of these therapies. It was nothing he was trained to do. We were crushed. The ray of hope he offered was this. He would prescribe, so that health insurance would pay for, any legitimate therapy that would not pose a medical risk to our son. He couldn't go into the unknown territory with us, but he would not stand in our way.

****

We were lucky to live near a world-famous university that houses a child study center. Some of the literature that my wife had collected suggested that this was a place where specialists could diagnose developmental disorders. We felt that once we could put a name to our son's issues, we could begin to effectively deal with them.

The child study center was in an old building in the downtown of the nearby city. As we waited to be seen by the doctor, we noticed the other children with their parents in the waiting room. In our rural home I had forgotten what a white-bread, two-parent, stereotypical family we were. Here we saw a lot of single mothers. We saw children who had very obvious issues. Some were screaming without stopping. Others had obvious physical impediments. Some were very lethargic. We felt a deep sadness, empathy with them, and sympathy for them. Our son seemed so unafflicted in comparison. Were we in the right place?

Eventually, we were called in to see Patty, a young, attractive grad student. She would administer a number of standardized tests to our son. This was the first of a great many such tests he would take over the coming years. I'm sure that there is science behind these tests, but they seemed so impersonal. They tested his recognition of familiar objects. They tested his vocabulary, his coordination, his ability to manipulate objects, to distinguish between similar objects, to group like items, to deal with spatial relationships and on and on. These tests took hours and we completed them in the course of several visits that became routine to us.

Finally, the big day arrived and we were sitting in a room, waiting for the doctor to come in and give us the answer. Our son played behind us with the toys they had there. As we were waiting, Patty, who had prepared all of the test results, spoke to us. She told us that many of our son's abilities were appropriate for a child of his age. Others were more typical of younger children. This was unsettling. Patty spoke about his lack of ability when it came to communication and his limited ability to attend to a particular task. His limitation in focus and attention were not appropriate for a child his age. I remember getting a hot tightness in the pit of my stomach. I kept waiting for a diagnosis. After she had read what seemed like a laundry list of deficiencies, she looked up and saw the effect her words were having on us. We were almost in tears.

Then Patty smiled. She began to tell us the things she saw in her time with our son that were promising. Each time he had come in to be tested, he had lasted longer before becoming resistant or bored. This showed he learned to adapt well. And she told us she could tell how much attention and love we had given him. How could she know this?

Patty said that each time she completed a section of testing, she would clear away the papers and other items and he would tell her, "Good job!" She said he had to have learned that through our positive reinforcement and that showed that we must be nurturing parents. This was important because my wife and I wanted to know where his disability came from. Was it something we did or didn't do? Was it genetic? Was it the one cup of coffee my wife drank during pregnancy or the partying I did in college?

Then Patty said something that has always stuck with me. She said that they see a lot of children at the center. They often find that they can only rule out certain diagnoses and can't really put a label on every child's condition. Then she said that she was sure that our son was not autistic. This was the first time

I had heard the dreaded "a-word" in connection with our son. It was shocking to hear the word, but a relief to learn that it did not apply. I asked how she could be so certain. She smiled. She said that she had caught him making eyes at her, flirting with her, several times throughout the testing. Patty said he was doing it right then. We turned around and our son was smiling at her. She said an autistic child would not do that.

Dr. Klausen entered the room and began his more clinical appraisal which was really just a recast of what Patty had already told us. Since they had ruled out all of the things they had names for, his diagnosis was PDD-NOS which stood for Pervasive Developmental Disorder – Not Otherwise Specified. Based on what he told us, it seemed like a fancy way of saying "we don't know". We were underwhelmed. We were ready to do whatever it took to help our son get over or around or through whatever this thing was and the experts could only tell us what it wasn't. How could we fight it? What could we do? Dr. Klausen said that some people chose to "go the drug route". Through trial and error, you might find a "silver bullet" drug that would trigger a breakthrough and clear the way for normal development. Or you might not.

The other route was therapy and education. The things that were not coming naturally to our son could be taught to him. He could be taught to attend and to focus and to communicate. He could be taught to decode and encode ideas into speech. It would be a laborious process and most public schools were not very good at this. We would have to support this educational process at home. In order to get these services from the public schools, we would have to present the school with a diagnosis. That is where the PDD-NOS label came in. Was such a vague diagnosis useful? Dr. Klausen told us that some of what he saw in our son was similar to some aspects of autism, but that the label of autism carried with it such a stigma and that most schools did not know how to deal with it. He didn't feel it would benefit our son in the long run to be labeled in that way.

And he recommended family psychotherapy. This long road we were already on could take its toll on our marriage and our family. Psychotherapy was a must. We were incredulous. Here the prestigious child study center had given us a vague, catch-all diagnosis and then told us they could not help with treatment. That would be up to the us and public school system. But, oh, by the way, our family needs a shrink. On the ride home, I looked at his business card. His title was "Licensed Psychiatrist" and I remembered what my cousin, a brain surgeon, once told me. If you go to a physical therapist with a bad leg, you'll get physical therapy. If you take the same leg to a surgeon, you'll get surgery. Specialists tend to view everything through the lens of their specialty. In the end, you are your own doctor. It's up to you to decide the path you take.

At the time, I was crushed that this famous child study center didn't have a miraculous cure for our son. The road ahead seemed uncertain. It was only later, as I looked back at our family videos of those days, that I saw the miracle. For us, the perceptible interruption in the workings of the laws of nature was that none of our son's differences made a difference in how we loved him. As statistically unlikely as it might have seemed, none of them made his birth anything but the most beneficial event ever in our lives. And, yes, we felt it all was being brought about by divine intervention. He was our miracle.

As I understand it, autism, or autism spectrum disorder, is a condition that is characterized by certain "symptoms" displayed by an individual. On one end is the "neuro-typical" or average condition. On the other end is an individual who is totally cut off from the outside world, isolated from social contact, non-verbal, perhaps repeatedly "stimming" (performing self-soothing behaviors such as rocking back and forth or waving of the hands). Between those two extremes is an infinite range of conditions, behaviors, and levels of performance. Some improve with treatment. Some, sadly, do not. Some are barely noticeable unless you know what to look for. Some are passed off as minor personality quirks or shyness. Some are incorrectly viewed as indicative of low intelligence or worse. I believe that some of these conditions are multi-layered. Some aspects are readily treated through education, various therapies and even diet. But every case is different and every case is a person who has something to offer us all. We are all different. Some of us are just a little more different. We all benefit from love and understanding. Some of us just need a little more.

2

WHAT DO WE HAVE HERE?

WHEN I was receiving emergency response training, a grizzled old veteran responder told the story of his first train derailment. He was being driven to the scene of the derailment and, as they crested a hill, the scene of the emergency was laid out below them. Dozens of railroad cars were flipped and twisted and strewn across the landscape. There were spills and fires and injured people. The old man said he turned to the driver and said, "I thought you said this was a derailment. This is nothing but a goddam train wreck!"

When one is trying to size up a situation, there is a temptation to try to apply previous experience and liken what you are seeing to what you have seen before. If you can make this new set of circumstances somehow seem like something you know, then dealing with it is not so daunting. You can tell yourself that you have succeeded with this sort of thing before and proceed as if this is routine. We do this to avoid having to face the unknown. There is fear in the unknown. And it can hold outcomes that we dare not consider. But if you want to deal with a situation to the best of your ability, you have to look unblinking at what is really there. Where does this begin and where does it end? What is it really?

My wife had been telling me off and on that she feared our son was not developing along the same path our daughter had three years earlier. She was such an involved parent. She never allowed our kids to sit idly. She was always reading a story, or reciting a nursery rhyme, or acting out some little scene with them from one of their favorite videos or movies. I was so much less involved. When I came home from work, I would spend time with the kids playing with the doll house or the toy cars or rough-housing giving "pony rides". And our son played appropriately with me. He was such a happy little boy and he loved his sister and played well with her. Nothing seemed to be wrong to me.

When I would ask him a question, he seemed to understand what I was asking. He would respond with a simple verbal reply of a word or two or an action. Sometimes he would respond with a full sentence or more. I had a hard time seeing what my wife was seeing. I was being fooled. Eventually, I came to understand that his longer utterances weren't original thoughts that he was composing. They were "scripts", bits of dialog or narration from the videos and movies that he had watched. He had a library of scripts in his head that he would "play" when he was asked a question. Often, the script was somewhat appropriate. Other times it was a non sequitur. But his use of scripts kept me fooled for quite a while. I resisted the idea that he had any significant learning or language problem. Finally, my wife told me that if I wanted to help, I would have to see what was actually there. I needed to spend time with him like she did.

So one evening, we turned off the videos and movies and he and I sat alone, away from his sister. We had a book and I

Getting My First Hug

started to ask him questions about it. There was a picture of a red ball.

"What is this?" I asked.

He looked at me. I tapped the picture and asked again, "What is this?"

I waited. No response.

Finally, I said, "It's a ball!"

"It's a ball," he said, only his declaration trailed off at the end as if he wasn't really sure.

"What color is the ball?" I asked. I had seen him name colors out of a book that had colored squares. I had seen him appear to correctly name many colors.

"Color is the ball..." he repeated.

"No, tell me the color of the ball," I said, trying not to sound more urgent.

"Color of the ball..." he repeated.

"The ball is red. What color is the ball?" I asked again. Surely, now that I had given him the answer, he would give it back to me.

"Color is the ball..." he offered weakly. He was not enjoying this activity.

I put aside the book and looked him square in his angelic face. He would not look straight back at me. He gazed to the side.

"Are you a boy or a girl?" I asked. I had seen him identify boys and girls in books and in videos.

"Boy or a girl..." he replied softly.

"No. You are a boy. I am a boy. Right? Are you a boy?" I am sure I sounded insistent at this point.

"You a boy..." he offered quietly.

I hugged him and told him I loved him. I took out the toy

cars and we played with them. We lined them up and counted them. I think I was reassuring myself that he was quite capable of a lot of normal play. But my mind was racing to try to figure out what was going on.

Later my wife introduced me to the concept of "echolalia". Our son was echolalic. When he didn't have a script to recite, he would repeat the last thing said to him. This was a symptom of autism, as was a lack of eye contact and, in some cases, the use of scripts. It hit me hard that my wife had been putting the pieces together for weeks and months, while I had ignored and denied what was actually happening. There was a part of me that thought that now that I knew this, I could quickly engage with him and fix it.

I had considered our son's playing with toy cars to be proper imaginative play. I began to look more closely at how he played with them. He would line them up, end to end, on the floor across our long basement. Sometimes he would count them, but always he would lay on the floor and sight down the long line of cars. He seemed to get some pleasure out of seeing that long line recede into the distance. We learned that this was a common behavior of autistic children too. He would sight along any long unbroken line. A counter, the toy box lid, the coffee table all had long straight lines and he would place his head down and look down along the lines.

The activities he enjoyed doing, he would do for hours. At first, I had seen this as a blessing. It was so much easier to keep an eye on him when he spent the afternoon lining up his toy cars and then collecting them and then lining them up again. All the while, he would sing a song or talk to himself. He was actually reciting scripts, sometimes spoken, other times musical from TV, videos or movies. Sometimes I would decide to intervene and suggest another activity such as drawing. He would whine and cry until I left him alone to go back to his cars.

When I reported this back to my wife, she introduced me to the concept of "perseverative behavior". This was something commonly seen in autistic children. I was catching up to where she had been for some time. She had seen all these behaviors in him, but I had not been ready to hear about them. Denial can be a pretty powerful force.

As I came to grips with the notion that our son had a learning and language development issue, I began to spend my time with him in a different way. I could not ignore it any more. I would try to gently interact with him as he watched his favorite videos or played with his cars and trains. I noted that he rarely looked at me. He knew I was there and he would let me play as long as I was enabling his play, his way. He did not take suggestions well. When I had been with him for a long while, I would ask him for a hug. He ignored the request. When I took him in my arms to hug him, he would whine and cry. This hurt me a lot.

Again, I told my wife how I could play in parallel with him, but that he would not acknowledge me as a person and never hugs me. She told me that social isolation was part of autism too. Looking back, there had been times when he was eighteen months to two and half years when these symptoms were not as noticeable. But they were becoming more noticeable and there was a regression in his social and verbal behaviors. Things were getting worse. And I was becoming very afraid.

What must the world be like for him? Unlike our daughter, who bloomed out into the world exploring and finding new things to experience and to love, our son was lock into a limited course of repetitive play by himself, perhaps beside but never with anyone else. And the only person he had a desire to be with was his mother. What if even that went away? What if that got worse? Where would this end? What could we do? This was like nothing I had ever seen before.

I was educated to be an engineer, a professional problem solver. I had been confronted with a multitude of problems in my workplace. Sometimes, as you uncover the problem, the solution presents itself. Or at least clues to the solution do. Those kinds of problems can be exhilarating. They are like a jigsaw puzzle. You can sort the pieces and try to put together a solution systematically. Or you can just start trying to hook one piece together with every other piece in turn until you find one that fits. Brute force. The other approach is to find another problem you know how to solve that is like the new problem in some way. Use previously successful methods and succeed again. Then there were the other kind of problems, the ones where you have no puzzle pieces, the ones that are unlike any problem you have seen before. Those kinds of problems are scary. When confronted by one of those, it's easy to become discouraged and want to give up. But we couldn't give up. The stakes were too high. Failure was not an option.

The secret to solving the kind of problem where you have no prior experience to draw on and no clues to start with is to turn to another engineer, another problem solver. And it's best if you can find one who is smarter, more determined and at least as invested in solving the problem as you are. Fortunately, I knew of such a problem solver. I was married to her.

****

Keeping in mind that I am not a doctor and I am not

giving medical advice, here's what I have learned about autism. It encompasses a wide spectrum of behaviors and conditions. And those behaviors and conditions may be present in the affected individual in a manner so subtle that perhaps everybody is on the spectrum. Or they may be present in crippling ways that stifle development. In a broad sense, autism is a developmental disorder affecting socialization and the ability to communicate. Often individuals with autism display certain repetitive behaviors. I do not know what causes it and I don't think anyone else does either. I believe every person on earth is unique and that goes for the people on the spectrum.

There is a philosophical question about the extent to which autism is a "problem" to an individual. You may hear people say that the single-minded focus of an autistic individual serves them well by eliminating distractions. And that may be true. I have met individuals on the spectrum who have exhaustively studied certain fields and have encyclopedic knowledge that may be very useful in business, art, or Trivial Pursuit. But there are also, generally, undesirable characteristics too. The time spent focused on, or accumulating information about, a single subject was likely spent alone and at the expense of becoming more "well-rounded". And many of the people I know on the spectrum have isolated themselves from the human contact that they need and want, yet do not know how to seek out.

There are, in some cases, additional conditions that may burden individuals on the spectrum. I am familiar with sensory integration as one of these. More about that later.

There are many other very serious conditions that I know very little about. I urge anyone who cares about an individual on the spectrum to seek out as much information as possible on the symptoms you see presented. Reach out to the support organizations in your area and utilize every resource at your disposal. And do it as soon as you can. Most experts (and I) agree that early intervention is the key to the best outcomes. There is a world of resources available now. And testing and treatment options abound. My wife and I were groping for answers twenty years ago that are a click of the mouse away today.

And I must mention that I have had no experience with individuals on the spectrum who have intellectual disability, violent behaviors directed outward or towards one's self, complicating physical illnesses such as digestive or sleep disorders or any other conditions that may accompany and complicate the already difficult task of helping that afflicted individual. My heart-felt prayers and sympathy are with these individuals and the people who love and care for them. They fight an uphill battle every day without any fanfare or recognition. Their stories are rarely heard and their true heroism goes unnoticed. And they are all around us, almost invisibly.

****

We could break down our son's issues into social, communication-related, repetitive (or perseverative) and sensory-related behaviors.

Socially, we could see that our son did not engage with others outside the family. Sometimes he would only engage with his mother. And there were times when he would barely engage with her. This was frightening. The vision of "classical autism", of an individual so withdrawn into himself that he could not relate to the outside world, was very scary to us.

Communication issues were classified into decoding, cognition (understanding) and encoding language. Our son would sometimes not respond to our requests and comments. There were times when it seemed there was an impenetrable wall between us and him. It was as if he could hear a faint noise, but couldn't begin to understand that it was communication aimed at him. And he had great difficulty putting his thoughts into anything beyond the most basic of words. There were times when I sensed he had something he wanted to say, but that damned wall was there preventing him from even trying to reach out. And many times when we were talking to him, we got the sense that the words were just "white noise" to him, without meaning.

We saw perseverative behaviors. He would do the same things over and over. He would spend hours lining up his toy cars on the floor, lay his head down beside the line and "sight" down it like a carpenter looking down the edge of a board to see if it was straight. And there was a succession of "obsessions". These were areas of interest that we chose to nurture, hoping that narrow interests might widen into curiosity about the larger world and foster communication.

Finally, his sensory issues involved tactile, visual and auditory integration. In neuro-typical development, the flood of information from the senses to the brain is miraculously integrated to form a cohesive picture of the world around us. Our brains use that picture to direct our behavior and improve our understanding. When that sensory information is not automatically integrated into the model our brains build, there is a disconnect that stifles understanding and hinders the development of many behaviors.

Social Skills

When our son was very young, there was a stage where our

goal was to get him to engage in something, anything beyond the simple perseverative tasks that he seemed to enjoy. The key to this first step was the TV. When we watched TV with our son, we noticed that there he seemed to engage in two different ways. The first was mostly passive. He would watch a tape of Sesame Street and perhaps sing along with a song or two. And when the tape ended, he would rewind it and watch it again.

The second mode of watching TV was more active. Our son had a noticeable interest in trains. Thomas the Tank Engine was his favorite show. He loved to watch the locomotives chug around the make-believe town and he quickly memorized all their names. He incorporated lines and phrases he heard on the show into the scripts he would use in place of original speech. Often he would use these scripts appropriately. Sometimes, less so. But his interest gave us a way to engage with him. We could ask him about the engines, what their names were and what they liked to do. He would respond with one-word answers and scripts. Gradually, we were having little conversations with our son! We could introduce concepts like comparisons and qualitative judgements. Which engine is the biggest? Which engine is always grumpy?

We happily used his obsession with trains to open up his world as much as we could. Of course, you can only go so far with an interest in trains. Fortunately, he developed, through watching videos, an interest in dinosaurs. Again, we used his interest, and later obsession, with dinosaurs to trigger conversations about what all their names were, which time period they lived in and what they ate. Our son had no problem acquiring the specialized vocabulary needed to answer these questions. If he had an interest, his mind seemed to open up and absorb whatever information about that interest was available. We bought and borrowed books from the library. We got flash cards, models of dinosaurs and every video we could find. While much of his conversation about dinosaurs was regurgitation of facts and replay of scripts lifted from videos, some of it was his own combination of groups of facts. He developed opinions about dinosaurs and preferences. His personality was emerging as his world opened up.

Use of "obsessions" is generally encouraged by some "experts" (and me). It harnesses an organic seed of interest that the child has and allows it to grow. We saw our son "break out" of his very isolated world through nurturing his interests, whereas I do not know if we could have ever "broken in" through our own means.

Our son's obsessions transitioned from trains to dinosaurs to the St. Louis Cardinals to video games, to English comedies (Monty Python, Red Dwarf), to music, to video production. And at every step his interest in the larger world has grown.

Digression. - It is recognized by "experts" that there are several classical areas of interest for individuals on the autism spectrum. Trains, dinosaurs, aircraft, magic, sports facts and mechanical objects like clocks or watches are often cited. Some individuals, like our son, may graduate from one to another as a part of a growth process. Other individuals "get stuck" on one "narrow interest" or "obsession" to the exclusion of all else. Again, I am not a doctor and I am not giving medical advice. I urge the loved ones and caregivers to consult with qualified experts in autism and child development to determine how best to use or not use these interests to help a particular individual. - End of digression.

For most of us, on some level, interacting with people comes pretty naturally. Maybe it's because we've seen human interactions since our earliest memories. They are on TV. They are all around us. When someone says hello, you say hello back. When they ask how you are, you tell them you are fine. To fill the awkward silence, you might ask them where they are from, what they do or what their favorite song or movie or baseball team is. It seems like something we are all born with, but it's not. These are learned behaviors. And they can become pretty complex. Most of us have brains that figure out these patterns and allow us to participate in social relationships without even thinking about them. Not everyone is so blessed. Some people have to be taught this process and these skills the way one is taught how to speak a foreign language, systematically, slowly, painstakingly.

Before I figured this much out, I thought that all we needed to do was put our son into a social situation and he would just magically "figure it out" and we could check this concern off the list. We invited two boys from our son's class over to play on a blustery autumn Saturday. They were nice boys who seemed to accept our son as just another classmate. They started out playing on the swingset. My wife and I anxiously watched from a window. The boys played nicely, but we saw that the two invited guests interacted with each other whereas our son seemed to gravitate toward solitary play. It didn't appear that they were shunning him, he just didn't engage with them.

There are eye contact, body language and spoken cues that signal our desire to be together. This was something our son lacked. I wanted to make sure that they all had a good time and after they had been playing on our swingset for a while, I brought out a football and started passing it around to them. The invited boys were thrilled to have an adult to pass to them and they asked for long bombs and high arcing passes, challenging themselves (and me) and each other. They made up little games and ran and chased one another almost instinctively. Our son was happy to be part of the shouting and to watch the ball flying high. He tried to catch and throw and didn't do badly, considering his lack of experience. I got the feeling that the other boys had other friends, older brothers or dads who had played with them this way before. Our son had never enjoyed this kind of play before. But as we played, he became disinterested. Perhaps he saw that the other boys were a little better at catching and throwing. They weren't afraid to get hit by the ball or each other. Before long our son had returned to the swing and I was entertaining the invited boys.

I tried to reengage our son in group play, but he became whiney and seemed happier to play alone. This was a characteristic of our son. It was part of who he was. If it had only been an occasional thing, it would not have been as troubling, but we could see it as part of a pattern of self-isolation.

As for the invited boys, they were nice enough to our son. At age 7 or 8, they could hardly be expected to go out of their way to befriend another boy whose differences they probably saw as confusing more than anything else. As the years went by, our son became a bit more out-going. He would, it seemed, consciously decide to participate or engage with a group. (Often it was at the urging of his parents.) At these times, he would absorb some of social rituals of his peers. He might pick up a new slang expression or catchphrase of the day. Through trial and error, he would make attempts to contribute to a conversation. With luck, he would blend in. Other times, he might stick out as different and retreat into silent observation. Or his stamina would wane and it would be time to go home. We kept trying to put him into "safe" social situations like the church youth group or groups of boys we knew to be kind. And over the years, our son became more at ease and was able to fit in.

Much later, in his late teens and to this day, he has found internet social media and online video gaming to be an arena where he can find people who accept him and with whom he can continue to grow and develop socially. Of course, there are unkind people, "trolls" who cyber-bully, but they serve the purpose of teaching our son that one must be careful who one trusts. These are valuable life lessons too.

Language Development

Once we had started to see progress in our son's ability to construct sentences and to participate in conversations, we saw a simultaneous improvement in his apparent ability to understand spoken verbal information. However, this was often limited. He was able to digest and decipher shorter bursts of spoken verbal information but seemed to lose interest as the passage got longer. We also saw that repetition was very helpful to strengthen his understanding and retention of both written and spoken verbal information.

As we came to understand more about how our son perceived the world and how he learned, we began to ask for certain accommodations in his classrooms. We would ask that he be allowed to sit at the front of the classroom near the teacher. This allowed him to absorb the presented material more readily and allowed the teacher to see if he seemed to understand. This was not always easy as he would always say that he understood, not wanting to stand out from the other kids. Being at the front of the classroom also kept him free from some distractions and perhaps spared him from some undesirable attention from others.

Another accommodation was to have study guides given to our son. This reinforced the key points of the lessons and allowed him to zero in on what was important, and likely to be included on tests. These guides were also helpful to my wife and me in that they helped us to prepare our son for tests and to make sure he was actually absorbing the material and not just going through the motions.

Obtaining study guides and lesson plans also allowed us to "pre-teach" lessons to our son so that when he received the lesson from his teacher it was not the first time he was hearing about a given topic. This pre-teaching before the classroom lesson and review after it allowed our son to succeed. It was an approach that suited the way he learned best. Not every child learns this way, but I suspect that this approach would allow a lot of students to learn more effectively.

In a way, we had to develop a partnership with each teacher. Most teachers were very open to this, although many of them initially saw us as overly-protective "helicopter parents". They had been fooled by our son's ability to mask his differences. In particular, his second grade teacher was impressed after hearing him read aloud. The teacher told us he read "at grade level". After some comprehension testing, he revised this conclusion, when it became clear that our son was reading at a higher level than he was understanding.

Our son had a powerful memory. It allowed him to learn the ABCs, then to amass a large vocabulary. He was never a phonetic reader. He simply memorized a huge number of words. This resulted in his guessing, often incorrectly, at larger words that were similar to words he had memorized. But, by trial and error, he would simply add the new word to his relatively vast vocabulary. We were often shocked by his correct usage of very large or advanced words. We generally came across such words in videos or in books about one of the subjects in which he had an intense, but narrow interest.

Our son also had a strong desire to succeed and thankfully had the intelligence needed to do the work he was assigned. These were coupled with the opportunity to learn. These three items are essential if a child is to succeed academically. If the opportunity is not present, it does not matter that the child has desire and intelligence. And opportunity and desire, sadly, are not enough. There is a certain minimum intellectual "horsepower" required. And the child must have the desire to self-motivate or the opportunity is wasted and the intelligence is never brought to bear. This is true at every level of education.

Reading comprehension was the problem, or, more correctly, a problem. We began to see that there were a finite number of such skills that would have to be acquired. If we could provide the resources he needed, he would conquer them one skill at a time. We had to determine which specific language skill was missing or was weak and build it up. This was doable, but difficult.

Another skill we determined was missing was "inferencing". Our son could read and understand, for instance, that one of two boys was tired and could not eat, but he could not infer that the boy was "sick".

One of my misconceptions about "special education" was that there would be long periods where a skilled educator would sit beside our son one-on-one, observe him reading, and correct and remediate. I pictured hours on end where such a gifted educator would patiently work through each of our son's issues until he was reading at grade level and had no further disability. This educator would use humor and motivation and would get to know our son, how he learned and what worked for him. This teacher would compose exercises specifically for him and challenge him. They would endlessly pound against the walls of his difficulties until they crumbled one by one. This would be a long, hard slog. But they would become close friends as this mentor saw the potential in our son. As time went on, this person would become more efficient at getting at the specific issues our son would present. This person would draw upon years of education and experience with similar cases to teach with methods that would be effective.

I pictured Anne Sullivan tirelessly working with Helen Keller. What an amazing teacher this would be! How fortunate we were to have this tireless person working in our school system! Our family would be forever in the debt of this educator. Of course, this teacher did not turn out to exist. Perhaps somewhere there is such a teacher, but this is not at all what the public school system offered us.

When you go to a butcher, you get meat. When you go to a tailor, you get a nice suit. You get what they have on the shelf. Looking back, there may have been some shadow of the in-depth personalized program I described above, but the sad fact is that no public school system has such resources to devote to a single child for an extended period of time. And once you dilute this kind of resource, it becomes largely ineffective.

I don't recall when it struck me that "reading comprehension" was a compartmentalized skill that could be taught like hitting a tee-ball. Maybe it was at tee-ball practice. One of the neighborhood moms was a tee-ball coach and would take the kids aside, one at a time, and teach them to swing a bat and hit a ball. It sometimes took an hour with just one kid and sometimes took several sessions, but she turned all of those kids into little hitters of one level of skill or other, but hitters nonetheless. Maybe I could do that with our son and reading comprehension.

I eventually remembered back to my second or third grade days in Texas. The school district didn't have specialists to assist every kid with reading issues, but what they did have was SRA. SRA was a box that contained pasteboard cards. On the cards were little articles and stories. The level of difficulty was color-coded. I remembered aspiring to achieve "aqua", "olive" and "tan" levels. You would read the little story and then answer some simple questions about it. Then you would check your answers. You made a little graph of your performance. When you had done so well at one "color level", you got promoted to the next. I recall it being self-paced and self-contained and very finely graduated. Could I find an SRA for our son?

Thank God for the internet, even in its then-primitive form. A few searches revealed that Scientific Research Associates, SRA, had been subsumed into McGraw-Hill and was available for purchase. It was not cheap. The box of cards I remembered was $700. But this seemed like a tool that I could use to help our son in a meaningful way. Why had I been content for so long to sit on the sidelines? I don't know. But suddenly, I had a mission.

I recall a story about monkeys. They were trying to learn about primate intelligence. They hung a banana out of reach of monkeys, but gave them a box they could climb up on. They also gave them a stick they could use to reach up for the banana. The box was not tall enough to allow them to reach the banana. The stick was not long enough either. The monkeys would have to climb up on the box and then use the stick in order to reach the banana. The monkeys stalked around their cage frustrated until they got into a position where they could see the box, the stick and the banana all in one field of view. Then they would quickly move the box, grab the stick, climb up on the box with the stick and enjoy a delicious banana. In remembering SRA, I had just had my "banana moment".

My nearest SRA dealer worked out of his car. He met me in the parking lot of a Mexican restaurant outside of Hartford. I gave him a check for $700 and he opened up his trunk. I grabbed the box and we went our separate ways. To the security camera, it probably looked like a drug deal.

Starting that afternoon, our son and I would do one or two SRA stories every day. Although he was in third grade, we started at pre-first grade level. The stories were easy and he breezed through the questions. He advanced from red to blue to green as the weeks went by. We kept a graph. As the stories got harder and longer, the questions became trickier. Our son had to look back at the stories to find the answers. He figured out that he could look for the words from the questions and find where in the text the answers might be. From the choices offered, he could figure out the correct answer. He mastered this way of answering.

But then SRA threw him a curve. The questions stopped using the words of the story and started paraphrasing them. He would have to figure out another way to find what was being asked for. He would have to actually understand the meaning of the words, of the paragraphs, of the stories. The questions starting asking, not about facts, but about ideas. This was harder. We worked together. I would do some of the reading, but I had to make sure he was engaged. I would ask him factual questions as we read, knowing that SRA would ask him thematic questions. It was hard for him to understand what was being asked for at times. So I would paraphrase the questions. But he was tenacious. He would look at the multiple choice answers and begin to eliminate ones that didn't sound right or that were silly. He would narrow down the options and then guess. Since we went back over all the answers to tally his scores, he would see which guesses were right and which were wrong. It was through this combination of brute force memorization, repeated rereading of material, and deciphering the kinds of questions that could be asked about a short article that our son developed "reading comprehension". He became a little detective as he read. If a story dwelled on the color of the horse, it was likely that the color of the horse was going to be important at some point in the story. As the SRA stories became two-page excerpts from novels, he came to expect even plot twists and irony. He made similar progress with recognizing and understanding inferences.

We did SRA together for a couple of years. He became able to keep up with classroom work "with modification". This became the way he would get through school. Directions would be highlighted. He would be given guided reviews prior to tests. He got preferential seating. He would get extra time on tests. These accommodations kept him in the mainstream and allowed him to participate and be "just one of the kids" in the class. Eventually the SRA began to gather dust in the corner. We passed it on to another family. The $700 price tag for a miracle seems pretty reasonable, looking back. I did mention SRA to our son's teacher and the school administrators who showed minimal interest. They weren't going to buy an SRA and were not particularly keen on knowing about our use of it. I came to believe that some folks in the school system saw their jobs as being as much about administration as it was about education. Unfair perhaps, but that is what I concluded.

Sensory Integration - Tactile Sensitivity

I was slow to catch on to so many of our son's differences. In his pre-school years, I noted that he did not like loud noises. Who does? He would clap both hands over his ears. I guess he did it for less than thunderous noises and the dramatic way he did it was noticeably different from the other kids.

He was also very particular about his clothes. He always wore a white cotton undershirt and was very particular about any loose threads that might cause him discomfort. We would have to look very closely to find the smallest threads and cut them so that he would be comfortable in his clothes. Sweaters and other garments that touched his neck were particularly troublesome.

My wife sought help for his tactile sensitivity. Through the school's occupational therapist, she got a small plastic brush with fine, soft bristles. The idea was that our son would lay down and she would brush him all over with this brush. The tactile stimulation would ease his discomfort at the slight sensations that were such a bother to him. Over a period of a few weeks, it worked! Our son seemed to look forward to the massage-like sessions and the attention from his mother. I even did it for him a time or two. It was a wonderful thing to experience progress like this. This may have been the first of our sons "differences" that we are able to eliminate. It gave us hope that there could be a way to work through the other issues that we had begun to list. We were beginning to develop a game plan with strategies for getting beyond these differences.

Getting a haircut was another of the routine chores that

became a real challenge. When you think about it, a haircut is a sensory bombardment. First there is the barber, a person unfamiliar to the child who will touch them and direct them. There is a sheet that covers the child that is wrapped around their neck and restricts their movement. There is the sight, sound and feeling of scissors, clippers, combs, spray bottles, and hair dryers. All of this happens as other strangers sit and watch the child endure it all. Our son did not like the experience from the beginning. We tried to find a barber he would like and even ended up cutting his hair at home, but it was always an unpleasant experience for all concerned until he was old enough to simply deal with it. Some differences he simply outgrew.

Visual Integration

We became convinced that there was something to the theory of sensory integration. Whereas, a "neuro-typical child" just naturally dealt with tactile sensations that might be bothersome, our son did not. It seemed that if the tactile sensory messages were being mis-transmitted to our son's brain, maybe other types of messages were also. We found a "behavioral ophthalmologist" and sought his advice. Again there were more voluminous forms to fill out.

Digression. - At every turn, there seemed to be a requirement to fill out forms about our son's history. It is understandable that any caregiver would want to be fully informed about the individual to whom they were going to administer, but over the years my wife must have filled out hundreds of these. She always took great care to make sure they were accurate and up-to-date. Even in those days, the late 1990s, things were sufficiently computerized that it seemed to be crazy to have to fill out nearly identical forms over and over for every new therapy, every new expert, every new organization that we came in contact with. Moreover, many of these contacts would require testing. Our son has been subjected to countless standardized tests of every kind. Usually, they told us only what was not wrong with him. That could be comforting. But what we were always in search of, but never found, was a test that would give us a specific result and, by extension, recommend a specific course of treatment. Often, the results of these tests had only depressing results to offer. They might say, for example, that at six years of age, his expressive verbal ability tested at a four year old level. I found such information depressing and of limited use. If the resulting recommendation was further educational intervention, which we were already doing, what was the point of the exercise? But, if there was any chance that all this work and frustration and depressing information could possibly benefit our son, we were going to push forward. And we did. - End of digression.

The "behavioral ophthalmologist", Dr. Kiley, was a kind man who told us that he was a pioneer in this field and had been working for 25 years with young people who experienced just what we were seeing in our son. He told us that he saw signs right away that our son could benefit from his services. The first step would be to fill out voluminous forms about his history and present condition. Then there would need to be three sessions of testing. We pushed forward. Dr. Kiley said that our son would need special glasses with prisms in the lenses and would definitely benefit from vision therapy. He saw as significant that our son leaned forward when he walked. We had seen that he was not the most athletic of boys, and this seemed like a scientific quantification validating our observations.

Dr. Kiley performed a number of very unique tests. One involved our son looking through a device that presented one image to his left eye and another to his right eye. He was told to draw what he saw. Later, the doctor took my wife and me aside and showed us what our son had drawn. It was supposed to be a sort of straight-lined version of an hourglass on its side. He had drawn seemingly random patterns. Dr. Kiley said that in 25 years of practice, he had never seen a patient struggle to that degree with that test. We were initially alarmed to hear this, but he reassured us that he could successfully treat such a condition. He also had our son read passages from a book as the doctor carefully observed him. Dr. Kiley told us that our son was the most remarkable patient he had ever observed.

Although the reading was slow and sometimes inaccurate, he had gotten through each passage. The doctor told us that the way most people read is by executing, without thinking about them, a series of exacting steps. First, one must acquire the word to be read with the eyes. Then, the word must be decoded. Then, the word must be released and the next word to be read acquired. Normal readers do this without thinking about the steps, in a fluid way so that the decoded words are held in the brain so that meaning can be assigned to phrases, sentences, paragraphs and so on. Our son, he told us, had to work harder than any patient he had ever seen at the individual tasks of acquiring each word and then releasing it to acquire the next word. Dr. Kiley marveled that our son could read without becoming exhausted. But he said it was no wonder that the boy had difficulty assigning meaning to what he had read. The mechanics of reading were fully utilizing all his concentration. Dr. Kiley gave our son exercises to do. Some of them involved us pointing to sequential or random numbers on a number line and having our son call out the numbers. Then we would do this with letters. This allowed him to build up his ability to rapidly acquire and release the characters. Other exercises involved following a swinging pendulum without moving his head or tracking a moving object in flight and touching it with a finger, like popping soap bubbles. We believe that these exercises benefitted our son's ability to read and understand what he was reading. But it was a long, slow process linked to other processes such as deciphering the meanings of words.

We continued to see Dr. Kiley for over a year. Our son wore glasses with prisms, but they did not seem to create any major effect. In time he came to dislike the glasses and we discontinued their use. We felt we had gotten as much benefit as we could from vision therapy.

Audio Integration

At about the same time we felt we were getting some positive result from the visual integration therapy, we took our son to an audio integration therapist. This was an analogous form a treatment that sought to help patients make sense of what they heard. There were times when we felt that our son was hearing instructions or directions but not understanding what was expected of him. We hoped this therapy could help. Unlike other therapies, this was done over a relatively short time frame and was not an open-ended course of treatment. Unfortunately, the course of treatment involved an hour in the morning, followed by an hour in the afternoon. And since the place of treatment was not local, it occupied an entire day. This was repeated for five days. Again, they wanted many forms filled out in advance of treatment. These therapies require an extremely high level of dedication on the part of the parents, or other caregiver. I cannot say enough about how fiercely indefatigable my wife was through our son's entire childhood. She never wavered in her commitment to his achieving his full potential. As his father, I shared the desire to see him succeed, but she did the heavy lifting. She filled out all those forms, again and again. She found and drove to the therapists. She waited in the waiting rooms. She coaxed and bribed our son to play along. He is to be praised for good-naturedly performing so well through so many of these therapies. I stand in awe of the two of them and the amazing results they achieved.

About the waiting rooms. One evening I came home from work and asked about the audio integration therapy. My wife told me about how our son had done so well. But then she told me about the other people she saw in the waiting room. As was always the case, we saw so many people who were so worse off than we were. So many children and older individuals had multiple afflictions. Often, she said, it was impossible to tell exactly what the afflictions were. And the behaviors these afflictions caused were sometimes loud, or obtrusive, and sometimes meant that personal hygiene was an issue. She told me about the weariness she saw in the eyes of mothers who had obviously been dealing with severe issues in their children, or in their adult offspring who had so little ability to care for themselves. I listened to how enormously sad the lot of so many of these people was. And these patients were lucky enough to have a parent or caregiver to be there for them. Imagine the multitudes who have been institutionalized because there was no one. Or because their parents or caregivers had become exhausted or financially unable to provide this care. We wondered about what would become of the adult man, who seemed to be operating on a grade-school level when his silver-haired mother passed away.

My wife told me she hugged our son extra close that afternoon when they left. We were so blessed. In our darkest hours, we were blessed beyond the dreams of some of those people. This realization has never left us. We could never allow it to slow our efforts to bring our son to the highest level he could achieve, but we always kept those others, who could just as easily be us, in our thoughts, in our hearts and in our prayers. They say that if you are in a group and you all lay down your troubles for all to see, you will gladly pick up your own and carry on, once you see what others must bear. It is too true.

The audio integration therapy was done this way. Our son was sat in a comfortable chair and was given a set of headphones to wear. Music and other sounds are played through the headphone with the frequencies being filtered and manipulated in various ways according to the diagnosis of the patient. It is believed that a number of such sessions, a half-hour at a time, can allow the brain to better sort out meaning from the sounds the ears hear. This therapy is used for diagnoses other than autism, but claims a respectable success rate with those on the autism spectrum.

****

How successful was the therapy? This is a question that can be asked of all the treatments and approaches that we tried. And it is hard to answer for a number of reasons. As a scientist, one is taught to design experiments with a control. The control is an unaltered set of variables and is used to establish a baseline against which is compared the experimental runs. For any experimental run, only one variable should be changed so that any difference in results may be attributed to the single changed variable. Life is not like that. Every day is different. A child's mood varies throughout the day. Plus, as parents who wanted to help our child as quickly as possible, we were not content to try only one thing at a time. The clock was running. Every day our son got older and it seemed wrong not to go after every possible advance we could make for him.

In addition, progress may be made gradually over time. We sometimes yearned for the "silver bullet" that would "flip the switch" and turn off the symptoms and turn on our son's full potential. I don't think there is such a silver bullet in most cases.

The tactile sensitivity faded quickly after a few weeks of the "brushing" sessions. I would not dismiss the visual and audio integration therapies, but the results were not as clear-cut to me. It is possible that our son's hand-eye coordination improved as a result of the visual exercises, but perhaps he simply became more coordinated as he grew. He played tee-ball, soccer and basketball through those years. Maybe those activities played a part. It is impossible to tell.

You sometimes don't know the effect of a course of treatment because you only have one subject to work with. We will never know how our son would have developed had we not done what we did. Nor will we know how he would have fared if we had tried other things. This is the reality of it. And so we tried all the things we could that seemed to promise positive results without undue risk. More radical drug therapy and holistic healing did not seem appropriate for us.

We did go to a naturopathic doctor and received vitamin supplements from him. How did they work? It is hard to say. That is why I do not intend this book to provide therapeutic guidance to anyone. I can only tell you what we did and what we saw. We know medical doctors who chose drug therapy for their own children, rather than the more labor-intensive (in my opinion) diet and sensory integration therapies. It seems to me that most of the drug interventions address symptomatic relief rather than seeking to heal whatever root causes may exist. But I am not a doctor and I cannot address this question with any authority and I do not offer medical advice.

I have been asked where our son was on the autism spectrum. We believe that he was mildly afflicted, but it is hard to say. As many tests as he has taken, I don't believe any of them tried to objectively measure that. I recall one battery of tests that related his performance on the tests to the typical level of performance of children of a certain age. It is very hard to be told that your six year old has certain verbal skills of a child years younger. And it is hard to understand what that means from a practical standpoint. You may be read a laundry list of such test score-based conclusions that make you feel terrible and cause you to fear for your child's future, but what does it mean?

Years after we got that set of "results", I was in a parent support group and we were going around the room telling our stories. Some of the parents were wealthy and highly educated. Some were not. Some were well-spoken and knew all the latest terms and jargon and were up on all the latest literature on autism. Others were not. But all of the parents had one thing in common. They cared deeply about their children.

At great cost, all of them are making financial and personal sacrifices in hopes of benefiting their children. Some go into debt. Some marriages break up. Sometimes divorced parents put aside their differences for the benefit of their child! We saw one young man who had four parents in the group working for him! (God bless them all.) Some of the parents had gotten a late start down the path of trying to deal with autism for one reason or another. Others intervened early. Some are young and full of energy and others are older and beaten down from so many failed therapies and trials. But one man sticks out in my memory.

He was a few years older than me. He impressed me as a blue-collar guy. He spoke plainly. And he had an up-beat attitude that was rare. I remember his words.

"Our kids just have a delay. That's all. Six years. That's it. At 18, they are dealing with what most kids deal with at 12. By the time they are 24, they will be like 18 year olds. And as they catch up a little at a time, they will blend right in with the rest of us."

He was so sure. And for many kids, our son among them, I think he was largely correct. For others, depending on their affliction, I am not so sure. And how much the interventions and therapies play a role in that "catching up" is hard to say. We'll never know how these kids would have fared without loving parents who are willing to seek out the information and the treatments and to acknowledge the painful realities and to make the hard decisions. And what about the multitudes who don't have parents like that? We'll just never know.

3

There's Nothing Wrong With This Kid

I found myself at a strange intersection as I considered our son. It was the intersection of denial and acceptance. Denial is a powerful force that can be aided and abetted by well-meaning friends and relatives. Acceptance can seem like the adult thing to do. It has a parallel track that is appreciation.

Somewhere between the time when my wife had told me she thought there was a problem and when we began down the road to addressing it, there was a period when I tried to make myself comfortable denying that there was a problem and accepting and appreciating what a wonderful kid our son was. The denial was always subtly troubling. The acceptance and appreciationl is the greatest source of joy I have ever found.

To be clear, our son was never "a problem". The problem was one of language integration and social skills development. Our son was a pretty happy toddler and young child. He loved watching "Barney the Dinosaur" and "Thomas the Tank Engine" and dancing and singing along to a collection of VHS tapes we amassed. He had an infectious smile and to quote my dad, "a hearty laugh".

It became routine for me to come home from work and get down on the floor to play with him and his sister. I was the pony for them to ride. We drew pictures together. We wrestled and played all sorts of made-up games. I built towers with blocks and he and his sister would take turns knocking them down in comical and creative ways. He and his sister would play with little figures of animals making animal sounds and with a dollhouse acting out little scenes.

We had a large finished basement that became a huge playroom for many years. It was littered with collections of toy cars and board games and animal figures and books and art supplies.

His sister liked to play pretend and put on little shows. And he joined in, loving the attention and praise that came with each performance. The only difference between his performances and hers was the dialog each supplied. Hers was either original, drawn from a little girl's fertile imagination or adapted from a movie or TV show. His was more gibberish, with snippets of dialog he had seen her use moments before. And his performances were a bit more repetitious, but always delivered with gusto.

We lived in a very rural part of Connecticut where the houses were separated by dense woods. This allowed us plenty of privacy. So when the weather was warm, we would fill up a little inflatable pool on the back deck. The kids would splash and swim in it, usually without bothering with swimwear. If the little pool got boring, they would set up the lawn sprinkler and dance and play and run through its misty spray.

It was easy to forget our concerns about our son's language development when I watched him playing like any other kid would. And when family would visit and see him enjoying those activities, they would question our concerns and remark about how happy and handsome he was. And they were right.

I had a friend of mine over to watch a ballgame on TV. As we watched, my son would run past the room we were in, jabbering to himself as he carried toys from one room to another. Sometimes he would come in to see what we were doing. My friend would greet him warmly and ask him for a "high five" and my son would happily oblige. I had shared some of my wife's concerns about our son's development with my friend. After receiving a big "high five" he would laugh and say to me, "There's nothing wrong with this kid!" He was being sincere and also trying to make me feel better. He was a father too and knew the hopes and fears that all parents hold for their kids.

We went on trips to local museums and zoos and took trips on the steam train that ran a few towns away. Our son showed interest in dinosaurs and trains. We took him to swimming lessons and made sure he participated in tee-ball, baseball, soccer and basketball. He didn't really like organized sports per se, but he enjoyed the excitement and feeling of accomplishment that catching a ball or scoring a run can bring.

It was certainly possible to selectively describe all of his interests and activities in a way that completely ignored his issues. And we did this for a long time. Even the most well-meaning of friends will tighten up and can't help but sound condescending if you allow that your child has a problem. We could sense, and our son could sense, when people were treating us with pity. And we never wanted that.

What was remarkable was the degree to which our son could fit into a group. He was so compliant and so able to adapt that he often "flew under the radar" of people with respect to his language and social issues. Many children are very accepting and uncritical of others who may be different. And many are so self-involved that they just don't notice subtle differences. If another child has under-developed language skills, it doesn't have any impact on playmates. Our son never acted out in any significant, noticeable way. He didn't attract attention. When the kids lined up, he got in line. When the kids got in a circle to play "Duck, Duck, Goose" he got in the circle and played too.

There were very few times when his differences would be exposed. We tried to make sure he wasn't the first to try a given activity so that he could model his behavior on an example. He was so good at doing that it seemed that he had heard and understood whatever verbal direction may have been given. Occasionally there would be children who would focus on our son. Perhaps they had noticed his echolalic speech or heard him respond inappropriately to a question. Such a child might express his curiosity which could have the effect of drawing unwanted attention to our son. This was rare but became more common as the kids got older. By the teen years, there were many who were quick to seize on any difference and point it out to others.

Our son's ability to adapt and model the behaviors of others to fit in was a mixed blessing. It allowed him to keep a low profile and be a part of peer groups. But it also fooled teachers and caregivers. They would see him behaving like all the other kids and assume we were being obsessively over-protective when we asked them to keep a special eye open for our son. In later years, it would decrease the needed services he would receive and make him more of a target for bullies. But I digress.

Another digression. - Our son got a lot of personal

attention from his mother all throughout his early years. We also allowed him and his older sister to watch TV, mostly educational shows like Sesame Street and Barney the Dinosaur. We had video tapes of nursery rhymes, Schoolhouse Rock, children's songs for every season and more. His sister's language skills had developed rapidly and we believe that was in large part due to the massive amount of verbal exposure she got from her mother and the additional exposure she got from videos. To this day we do not believe that our approach was detrimental to either of our children.

Our son always had a sense of what was expected of him, regardless of his ability to deliver it. From a very early age, he was able to adapt the skills he had in an attempt to do what was expected. A simple example would be lining up behind his peers and following the person in front of him. If each child put on a coat, he would put on his coat. We often had to instruct caregivers and teachers not to assume he truly understood a direction because he was so good at blending in and doing what he saw others do. This strategy worked very well for him in a great many situations. But it has its limits.

The use of scripts is not uncommon among some autistic individuals. These scripts are rote passages of verbiage that they can recite at will. This verbiage may come from things they have heard people say or they may come from recorded media. Our son's early speech was dominated by one form or other of scripts. That is not to say that the use of scripts is necessarily inappropriate. Most of us use some form of scripted verbiage every day.

We came to understand that the use of scripts was one way he adapted to not being able to formulate more complex ideas into his own words. And he was often very clever about which scripts he used and how he employed them. Sometimes he used scripts almost as a security blanket. He would recite passages from a video when he was playing. Our son loved Thomas the Tank Engine stories on TV. The distinctive Liverpudlian accent of narrator Ringo Starr or, later, the clear, friendly tone of George Carlin, were easy for him to pick up and store away as scripts. As he played with his toy trains, it was natural and appropriate that he would perform these scripts. Other times, we would ask him a question and he would startle us with a more lengthy verbal response than we thought he was capable of. Often we found that he was reciting a script. Sometimes he had chosen a script that was so close to being an appropriate answer and so natural-sounding that we were fooled. Other times, it was clear that he had just recited a random script. - End of digression.

Our son was happy and comfortable in our home and in situations that were or became familiar to him. He felt safe and able to perform at his best around his immediate family and a few playmates. In short, he was a lot like all of us. His cousins loved him and enjoyed his company. He was a happy kid who didn't make demands and enjoyed laughing and being silly. A lot like all kids. But the circle of friends didn't grow.

I don't know whether it's a symptom of these modern times or if it has always been this way, but making new friends did not come easily to our son. Part of it may be the innate or quickly learned rituals that are so important in meeting people and making friends. Friends act alike in many ways. They adopt the same mannerisms and words and behaviors. When we make new friends we seek out the common interests we may share and all the ways we may be alike. This familiarity is the beginning of friendship.

This skill of quickly ingratiating one's self with a new person did not come naturally to our son. To put a good spin on it, he was simply shy. In reality, he was becoming isolated. I can't blame the other children. And we are thankful for the kids who looked past the differences to reach out to our son.

In sixth grade, many of the lessons throughout the year built toward the big, week-long class trip to Nature's Classroom, a camp retreat where science, history and other lessons were brought to life. It's a sleep-over experience and we wanted our son to be part of it. I volunteered to chaperone and got to see how the other kids treated our son first-hand, really for the first time. It was a mixed bag. He wasn't being relentlessly bullied as I had feared. His male classmates were indifferent to him much of the time, which was fine. And they even encouraged and enjoyed his participation in free time dance-offs, silly impromptu performances in the cabins in the evening.

Our son wasn't picked to dine at the popular kids' table, but a group of very nice girls invited him to eat with them. It was sweet to see him treated so well. And sixth grade wasn't so far from the age when having female friends would be a very desirable thing indeed.

While I was pleased to see our son was not being openly ostracized, I was aware that, at least for that week, I was his closest friend. If I had not been there, I feared he would have experienced much of Nature's Classroom alone.

This experience and others led my wife and me to conclude that there were worse things than being shy. While we would have wanted our son to have a true friend or two, we were happy that school was not the torment for him we sometimes feared. We struggled to understand what the world was like for our son and how he was perceived by his peers. In the end, we, as a family, pulled tighter. We would provide all the love and friendship and experiences we could for him. In many of the most important ways, there really was nothing wrong with this kid.

There is a great temptation to wish for this thing or that for your child. But life is tricky and there are few "straight lines". Be careful what you wish for, they say. And it's true. There were times when I would see another kid on the baseball team or in the neighborhood and silently wish our son could be friends with him. Over the years, I have had such thoughts quite a few times. But in almost every instance, I later learned that the other kids, the ones who seemed like the ideal friends for our son, had issues of their own. Sometimes they were serious issues. I have learned that everyone has some challenge. Nobody is perfect. That realization has made me appreciate our son more than I can say.

4

The Way Forward

OUR pediatrician and the prestigious child study center were no help. My wife had a sheaf of Xeroxed newsletters from a handful of disparate organizations. She had been urging me to read them along with her for quite a while when I finally became concerned enough to do so. One common theme all the organizations espoused was that time was of the essence. Concerned parents could not and should not wait for medical science to study and develop cures for autism or whatever we wanted to call the symptoms we were seeing. The options for treatment were all over the map. Some of them sounded dangerous. Some of them were invasive. There was a lot of pseudo-science and folk medicine and alternative medicine being recommended. As an engineer and scientist, I was uneasy considering any of the non-traditional paths. But our doctor had basically left it to us. Medical science had, in my view, failed us.

My wife had been making notes. There seemed to be some kind of connection between diet and autism, at least in some cases. Some children were benefitting from supplementation and special diets. The supplements that were mentioned most often were substances that were found in nutritious foods. That did not sound too wild to me. And the diets were meant to avoid certain foods that a child might be allergic too. But our son wasn't allergic to anything. Or was he?

Science can be a contradiction. On one hand it constantly questions everything. The best thing about the scientific method is that the most respected and believed-in theory or model can be completely toppled by a lone individual armed with a single, irrefutable fact. On the other hand, science only recognizes its own. Things that are not purely science are often discarded or disregarded, I think, because science doesn't know what to make of them. Naturopathy is an "alternative" medical discipline. I'm not sure of what it is or isn't beyond that. But my wife had read that many autistic patients benefitted from naturopathic treatments such as diet supplements and it didn't sound like anything harmful, so I gave my blessing.

The naturopath prescribed something called DMG and an allergy test for our son. To this day I can't tell you what the DMG did or did not do for him. But the allergy testing was revelatory. Our son's diet consisted of bagels, peanut butter and milk. We'd get him to eat a little steak or chicken from our plates, but that was pretty much it. The results from the allergy testing reported allergies to, you guessed it, gluten (found in bagels), casein (found in milk), peanuts and beef. We were stunned. And confused. The allergy symptoms we had heard of were things like rashes, nausea, even difficulty breathing. How could bread and milk interfere with speech development? And what would our son eat if not these things?

The naturopath directed us to health food stores and we found that there were gluten-free, casein-free products out there. We took away the peanut butter and steak and replaced them with green peppers, lettuce, cucumbers and fish. And it was not just our son who went on this diet. The whole family did. We were advised that if we kept the forbidden foods in the house, he would find them. If he saw us eating them, he would feel punished. It would just be simpler if we all did it. And so we did.

I don't wish to sound ungrateful. I was glad there was a gluten-free, casein-free cookie mix, so that our son could have cookies at nursery school and kindergarten when the other kids had a snack. But in the early 1990s, those mixes weren't as tasty as one might want. The brownie mix was little better. But when that is all you have, you make the best of it.

We had been on the diet for about six weeks when we began to notice something remarkable. I was watching TV with our son and he did two things he had never done. He turned to me and said, "That man is funny." He had put four words together in a coherent sentence. Was this a script? Was I being fooled again? Maybe. But he had also acknowledged me and shared this thought with me. That is a social interaction. And I couldn't recall him initiating any such interactions with me before. I was joyful.

As the weeks went by and our consumption of the bland brownies and the flat less-than-delicious cookies, as well as fish and veggies, increased so did our son's "length of utterance". Soon three- and four-word phrases became common. At dinner each night my wife and I would recount the latest sentence he had come out with. Eventually, he put sentences together. We were moving forward. We were moving out of the darkness and into the light. I prayed that the progress would continue or at the very least that he would not regress.

At about the same time, my wife suggested that we try another "alternative" therapy. There was something called "secretin" that had produced amazing results in some cases. Secretin is a hormone that the body produces that controls certain processes of digestion. There was a story that a non-verbal autistic child had developed severe digestive issues and received a secretin "infusion". On the way home from the doctor, he spontaneously began talking for the first time in his life! This was every parent's dream! Could it be true? Might there be a "silver bullet" out there?

The use of secretin for the treatment of autism is an "off label" use. That is, secretin is not approved for such treatment. There were only two doctors in the country doing this treatment. And one was two hours away from where we lived. We were lucky enough to be granted an appointment with him. The first appointment would be for an examination. Then, if our son was deemed to be a candidate, there would be four weekly infusions. The drive to the office was long and filled with hope and tension. We dared not get our hopes up.

Life has a way of teaching you lessons when you least expect them. My mother used to say, " I was sad because I had no shoes, then I met a man who had no feet." On our worst day, we are still so blessed. It may be hard to see it, but it is true.

At the office, we waited with other parents and children. And we were once again made aware of how lucky we truly were. There were so many children who were suffering with multiple serious conditions. Some moved uncontrollably. Some moaned and cried. Some wore legs braces or other orthopedic devices. As we sat there with our son quietly playing with a toy car, we silently prayed. We prayed for our son, to be sure. But we prayed for the other children there and their families. I could barely look at them for fear I would break down. We entered the office feeling we were the family most in need of help and left feeling so grateful to only have our own problems.

The doctor was a kindly older man, exactly what you might expect. His white hair was unkempt, but his smile and voice were kind. He sat next to our son on the examination table and spoke quietly to him.

"You are a fine young man, aren't you?" he said. "You are a smart boy too, aren't you?" Our son did not pull away from the doctor as I expected him to. Instead he sat passively.

The doctor told us he would like to give our son an infusion right away. This would save us one four hour round-trip. We agreed. He took out a little vial of secretin and a little tube with a needle on one end. He connected it all up and gently put the needle in our son's arm. A few minutes later, he removed it. There were no tears. The doctor wished us well and told us to make three more appointments at one-week intervals.

We drove home. As our son sat strapped in his car-seat, we wondered if he would begin to recite Shakespeare or ask us about the meaning of life. We tried to make simpler conversation and got the usual disinterested grunts. There would be no flash of lightning or magical cure on this ride home.

My wife and son made the three repeat trips. They were much the same as the first had been. There was never a moment of instant cure. Our feeling was that secretin didn't work for us. But who knows? At about the same time we were in the early stages of our gluten-free, casein-free diet. And it was a few weeks later when we began to see progress that has continued, in many ways, to this day. So maybe the secretin did work. Or maybe it was just the diet. Or maybe it was the supplements or the DMG, that I poo-poo'ed. Who can say? Maybe our son would have begun talking more on his own without any of that.

We will never know for sure. But as parents, we had to do something. We had to do all we could. And we would never stop.

A few months into the gluten-free, casein-free diet, several weeks after the last secretin infusion we were feeling pretty good. Our son continued to connect words into sentences and sentences into little monologs. I have yet to tire of hearing him talk even seventeen years later. I remember sitting at the dinner table. He had finished his meal and was walking around in the kitchen. We were quizzing him on his day's activities, as we often did. It was to keep him "using his words" in a push to make up for lost time. I asked him about his trip to the park, about the shows he had watched on TV and about anything else I could think of. He was not only responding with non-scripted language, he was smiling. I did what I had done hundreds of times before. I leaned down and spread my arms wide and said to my son, "Come give Daddy a big hug and kiss!"

So many times before I had done that and seen no reaction. Or worse, he would pull back. But this time he looked at me and ran into my arms. I felt his arms wrap around my neck and he hugged me tightly. Tears poured from my eyes. He broke the hug and planted a wet kiss on my lips and then asked me, "Why are you crying? Are you sad?"

I told him, "You never hugged me before and I'm so happy. I'm going to need a lot more hugs, OK?"

"OK, Dad. Just don't be sad."

"I won't be sad anymore," I said. And that was one of the best moments of my life. Whenever I see our son, I think of that and I know that miracles are real.

5

Education and Expectation

TEACHERS can have such a profound effect on their students. A great teacher can inspire a student to pursue a dream. They can guide and shape young minds and help to find the things that ignite curiosity. To this day I can remember entire lectures almost verbatim from teachers who inspired me nearly forty years ago. The impact of a great teacher can go far beyond the subject matter covered in their textbooks. Great teachers teach about life, growth, overcoming challenges and realizing one's potential.

There are great teachers who are warm, encouraging and nurturing. And there are even great teachers who seem cold, tough and antagonistic. There are teachers you think you hate. It may be years before you can look back and see how much they truly taught you. The lessons we learn are often not the ones described in the course catalog.

Few teachers choose that profession to get rich. Many are humanitarians doing a difficult job because they love kids and are passionate about touching lives. We were lucky to run into some of those. Others taught us tougher lessons about overcoming adversity and getting what we needed from a dysfunctional system. I guess those were important lessons too.

We had enrolled our son in a popular pre-school program in town. It was a well-thought-of program run by a group of nice ladies. The curriculum consisted of arts and crafts, story time, creative play and field trips. Knowing how difficult some communication was for our son, we were nervous to see how he would fit in. After a couple of weeks, it became clear that his lack of verbal skills was noticeable and, at times, combined with his lack of social skills, troublesome. There was no great blow-up or scene. We just began to get reports that he was unhappy when certain activities ended. He didn't seem to understand the agenda and there was minor friction with other kids with whom he couldn't really communicate.

As we removed him from this program, we heard from the teachers words that we would hear for the next twelve years. The teachers loved him. They could see how he tried. They could see he was sensitive. And they wanted him to succeed. What they didn't say was that they just didn't know how to deal with a child who had the differences he did. This became a pattern.

But before despair could set in, my wife heard about a special needs pre-school at the local elementary school. There was a time when I would have bristled at the phrase "special needs", but as we were focused solely on providing what our son needed, I barely gave it a thought. I remember meeting the lovely lady who ran this remarkable program. She was upbeat and smiling and seemed to radiate good will. Her classroom was filled with every type of toy and there were children in every part of it engaged in creative play. If you didn't look twice you might not even notice that this one had two hearing aids, or that one was blind, or the other one was in a wheelchair. Once again, we were reminded how lucky we were.

And our son dived right in. The room was large enough that there was room and toys for all of the kids. After several classes, we asked the teacher how our son was doing. She said she was using him as a role model! He played mostly on his own, but would often have to share with another student. Sometimes he would even play in groups. It seemed that being around these other kids who had differences brought out the best in our son. She said he was kind and took turns and was considerate of the feelings of others. Our son loved this class and when his time there came to end, and it was time for kindergarten, we had mixed emotions. He had learned all he could in this safe space. It was time to go back to the real world.

Kindergarten in the public school was usually a half day, morning or afternoon. We wanted our son to have as much exposure to the classroom routine and to other kids as possible. As much as we might have wanted to hold him close, we knew that to grow he would need to deal with others. So we enrolled him in the full day program. My wife was an in-class volunteer and so was able to keep a close eye on him. After his experience in the special needs pre-school, kindergarten was not too much of a challenge or adjustment. He did well. His teacher was a lovely young woman who told us how much she loved him, how hard she knew he tried and how much she wanted him to succeed.

This was about the time we had gotten the evaluation from the famous university's child study center with the diagnosis of Pervasive Development Disorder - Not Otherwise Specified (PDD-NOS). We thought long and hard about whether to bring this diagnosis to the attention of the school system. Did we want to label our son? To what extent would this stigmatize him? What was the benefit? It soon became clear. In order to get special services from the school system, you had to have a diagnosis. We wanted to take advantage of the specially-trained teachers who might have expertise in language development and social skills training. To do so we would have to put our cards on the table.

The public schools had a protocol to follow in such matters. They would form a Planning and Placement Team (PPT) and create an Individualized Education Plan (IEP) for our son. This all sounded great. A week or two into the school year we met with the principal, school psychologist, special ed teachers and our son's first grade teacher. They told us about all the services they could offer, but our son's homeroom teacher said she didn't really see that much need for these services in our son's case. He seemed fine, perfectly normal. She had been fooled by the way he could adapt and fit in. As much as we loved hearing how normal our son was, we knew there was much work to be done. He would need to be evaluated.

There was a week of testing that followed and a report was generated. It detailed and quantified what we already knew. He had language and social skills deficits. He needed services. At the next PPT meeting, attended by an officer of the school district, the IEP was presented. Our son would get 8 eight hours of service from a trained language pathologist and 8 hours of service from a therapist skilled in development of social skills. These services would be delivered to him in his classroom so he would remain a part of the mainstream as much as possible. It sounded wonderful. Just what he needed.

What we soon found out was that there were other students in his class who also had IEPs and who also got such services from the same specialists during the same time period. So the reality was that our son got the partial attention of these specialists when they weren't dealing with the other children. Not so wonderful.

There were periodic PPT meetings and each of the teachers and specialists and administrators would say positive, optimistic things about our son and his progress. That was uplifting. But the goals of the IEP remained "in progress". The year wore on until magically, at the final PPT meeting for first grade, all of the goals were "satisfactorily achieved"! We were happy on one hand, but we could see that significant language and social gaps remained. When we expressed our concern, we were told he would need to be evaluated again. And the cycle would repeat.

And what would happen during the summer? Surely, the PPT would want to keep the momentum going and build on the "achievements" of the past nine months, right? Yes. The PPT recommended a wonderful summer program of intensive language and social programs. These would be individualized and our son would receive much more attention than he had during the school year. It sounded too good to be true. It was. The catch was that although the PPT recommended this program, there was no one available to administer it. All the teachers and specialists were going on vacation! Maybe, they offered, our son could participate in the town's rec department camp.

We were crestfallen. The progress that was reported seemed suspect. The achievement that was reported seemed dubious and ephemeral. The summer seemed like it would be a time of lost momentum and backsliding. Oh, and the PPT was losing one specialist to maternity leave. Another one was moving. There would be a new teacher for second grade, of course. And the school was getting a new principal. In other words, next fall we would be back to square one. But every member of the PPT said how much they loved our son, how sweet he was, how hard he tried and how much they wanted him to succeed. And they all seemed to mean it.

And so it would go for the next twelve years. There were endless evaluations. Our son has taken more standardized tests than a platoon of college-bound juniors. We have reams of IEPs, a set for every grade. And they all show an amazing change in the last reporting period of each year from goals "in progress" to goals "satisfactorily achieved". Every summer there were recommendations for a great program that never materialized. And every new year the goals were reset by a new team and the cycle repeated itself.

We did try sending our son the the town rec department camp. It was run by a poorly-paid staff of mostly teen volunteers and served as summer childcare for most of the attendees. A child with special needs got no special attention and was relegated to the back of the pack. Our son begged us not to send him back. We even paid a neighborhood teen to "shadow" our son and act as a lifeguard. It was no different that year.

What we came to see was that the public school was doing all it could given its limitations of time, talent and funds. The PPT/IEP system was put in place to be a demonstrable, legally defensible mechanism to show that some attention had been paid, some effort had been made and some progress, however nebulous, had been achieved for every student with a diagnosis. Each teacher knew his or her commitment to a given student would only last for one year. The specialists might stay on the case longer, but the type of language and social dysfunctions our son had, and consequently objective progress in treating it, was hard to measure.

The goals and targets remained much the same from first through twelfth grade.

> He will ask and answer concrete questions.
> He will ask and answer abstract questions.
> He will initiate spontaneous conversation.
> He will maintain conversation.

To be fair, real progress was made. Our son's language and social skill did improve over these years. How much credit should go to the public school's programs is impossible to determine. It's like the diet, the secretin and the DMG. Would the progress have been made without them? Who knows? And there was never a goal of making a friend.

Our family pulled tighter over these years. Our daughter had a typical, better than average experience in the same school system. She did what she could for her brother, but being three years older, their time in the same school was limited. I would take time from work to be at the PPT meetings. My wife did the lion's share of the work. She drove our son to school, presided over the never-ending evaluations, studied the IEPs, and never stopped looking for new ways to help our son.

I would be remiss if I did not acknowledge the excellent teachers that helped our son. There were some. Some of them took an extra interest in him. One taught him chess. One taught him to play the baritone horn. One taught him computer skills. Another one taught him to make and edit videos, a skill that may end up being his life's work. And the affection that many of them expressed was real and not without value. We appreciate all of that.

In the end, the public school system is just that, a system. They have a limited staff, limited skills and a limited budget. They may have done for our son the best they could. It wouldn't be until the very end of our experience with them that the system's true colors would be displayed. And that was a lesson, not for our son, but for my wife and me.

6

Speaking of Sports

FOR an American male of my generation, sports was a huge part of growing up. For better or worse, it was a major part of how we determined who we were. I fondly remember my dad teaching me how to play baseball. He seemed as eager as I was to play "pitch and catch" as soon as he got home from work on warm summer afternoons. I can see him smiling when I caught a "high fly" and I can hear his change jingling in his pockets as he jumped to snag one of my many errant throws.

Sports provides an arena for triumph and defeat, for life lessons, and true drama. My dad was a frustrated athlete, the twelfth man on his high school basketball team who acted as equipment manager for a year until he was allowed to ride the bench and play "garbage time" minutes at the end of games whose outcomes were no longer in doubt. I know he wanted me to excel in the way that he hadn't. But I never did.

I played Little League baseball for several years and rec league basketball, both with little success. But my family, and my dad especially, was at every game to cheer me on. Dad even announced a few games on the PA microphone. He said he was so proud when he introduced my times at bat.

I can still see the disappointment in his face when I told

him I would never go out for any sports in high school. The jocks hated me, or so I thought. Why would I offer myself up for the hazing, ridicule and nonsense that I was sure was in store for me? Maybe he thought to himself that if his son wasn't to be a champion, perhaps his grandson would.

Our son never showed much interest in sports. When you look at televised sports objectively, there is a lot of talking using specialized jargon. The action is sporadic and the rules are sometimes Byzantine. Attending a live sporting event is a spectacle even to the non-sports fan, but to a boy with autism, the running commentary of televised sports is little more than noise.

However, physical fitness is unquestionably a worthy goal. And organized sports is the most obvious way to pursue it. And if you are looking to help a child fit in with his peers, being on a team seems to be the way to go.

The best thing about the youngest levels of sports is that all of the kids are about the same in ability. The practices and games are a joyful, barely organized chaos. Every kid has to be told what to do and how to do it. None of them know the rules. And while he-men jocks may bemoan tee-ball and "coach pitch" as being sissy-fied versions of the hardball they grew up with, these versions of the sport really provide a nice entry into the game.

So it was that we signed our son up for tee-ball and I volunteered to assist the coach, essentially to act as a lifeguard for our son. We didn't talk to the coach about our son's "special needs". It seemed that this was one place where they didn't matter. And it worked!

For two seasons of tee-ball and one of "coach pitch" baseball instructional league, our son played. And he held up the family tradition of being neither the best nor worst player on the team. It was a blessing that these leagues were "non-competitive". There were modified rules to allow each player to bat and to play each position. Again, I would say to the he-men who deride this form of sports, imagine if your son wasn't the chip-off-the-old-block alpha male. You would want him to have a chance. These leagues gave our son a chance.

The team experience was good. Teammates encouraged our son and he cheered them on in return. Coaches always had positive things to say and some took extra time with our son. The routine of practice and the ritual of games provided a form of discipline that was good for our son. And some of the time it was fun for him. He wasn't sad when the season was over, but he didn't fight too much when the next season rolled around.

Of course it wasn't all positive. Sadly, sports and competition, as muted as it was, brings out the worst in some people. There were coaches who, after attending the orientation meetings and hearing the presentation about how the league was for teaching and strictly non-competitive, kept score anyway. I remember before one game, as we exchanged lineup cards, one such lunkhead said, "So, three outs, nine innings and we keep score, ok?" He was asking if it was ok with our team if we violated the rules and purpose of the instructional league.

My son's coach replied, "The league president is right over there. Why don't you go ask him? Our team is going to bat around all six innings and the scoresheet stays blank. If you don't want to play that way, we'll accept your forfeit." I could have kissed him.

During the game that followed, I could hear the opposing team's players counting outs and keeping score. They also calculated their own batting averages and quietly jeered our kids. I was proud that our kids ignored them.

But as in any activity, the kids could see who was better, faster, and more skilled. And they could see who was not so blessed. And our son could see he wasn't the top player. It was hard to get him to play sometime, but the friendship of a few kids and the promise of post-game pizza usually worked.

Soccer season came after baseball. There is a lot less emphasis on individual performance in soccer and a lot more chaotic running around. Our son liked soccer a bit more than baseball. He had a flair for defense and stopping the ball. He got a few shots on goal, missing a couple of times by the tiniest of margins. We longed for him to have one of those "magic moments", a taste of personal glory, the thrill of victory.

Basketball came after soccer. We had a basketball goal in our driveway. Our son understood the rules and had some skills. The first two years he played, the kids were mostly so small that none of them really excelled. The games were short and all the kids got to play more or less equal minutes. I think our son enjoyed his time on the bench cheering on his teammates as much as he enjoyed playing.

Most of the games were low scoring and really only a few of the kids could make a basket with someone guarding them. Our son wasn't one of them. But it didn't seem to matter to him. He was ready for each season to end.

After he had played three or four seasons of baseball, and two or three of soccer and basketball, he asked us if he could end his sporting career. We have made it a rule that if he could articulate his feelings and why he wanted to do or not do something, we would generally give him his way. We agreed that this last season of basketball would be his "swan song".

Getting My First Hug

His team was pretty good. They seemed to have several kids who could score and they won most of their games. It was always more fun to win than lose. Although I had always coached or assisted on our son's baseball and soccer teams, I chose not to do that with basketball. I found I was becoming one of those parents who couldn't keep quiet in the confines of the gym and I didn't want to embarrass myself, my wife or our son. So I chose to sit up high away from the court and I even kept a towel to wring in my hands and sometimes chew on to keep myself quiet.

You see as time went on, our son was getting better. He gained confidence from the acceptance of his teammates. And the fact that they won a lot of games didn't hurt either. There were a number of games where our son had shot the ball and come within a bounce of scoring. I dared not say so, but I began to want to see him score more than anything. Each time he would heave up a shot, I would bite down on that towel and stifle my frustration. Game by game, he figured out how to get open down low, near the basket. And his teammates did not give up on him. They might pass to one of the big scorers more often, but they would not ignore our son when he was open.

The last game of the season came and we were in the big high school gym. This game would determine which team would make it to the playoffs. Both teams were good. There were a lot of parents there. This was real sports. I took my seat high up in the stands away from everyone with my wife beside me.

I gave that towel a real workout twisting it and chewing it throughout the first half. Our son took one shot that was just a fraction too high. I muffled my reaction into the towel. So close. I had reconciled myself that my son's sporting career was to be no better than my own, probably no better than my dad's. My dad had passed away about four years before. My heart still ached when I thought about how much he would have loved to see his grandson play basketball. If he had ever been disappointed by my performances he had never showed me anything but his pride. I could only imagine how he would be smiling to see his grandson play.

Early in second half, our son's team pulled ahead. They looked good and everything was clicking. They were passing the ball well and shooting well too. There was a loose ball under the opponent's basket and our son's team got the ball. Our son took off to a spot under their basket and waved for the ball. One long pass found our team's best shooter near the foul line. But rather than shoot, he passed to our son. Two defenders converged on him. He put up a shot. It hit the backboard, then the inside of the front of the rim and then dropped through the net! He had scored!

I erupted in a loud cheer, leaping to my feet. "YES!", I cried. "YES!" It was the greatest single moment of victory I have ever experienced. I jumped up and down with my fists in the air. I looked down and saw my son smiling. The euphoria was incredible. My wife and I hugged. I felt like years of work had paid off in that one moment. I pictured the endless hours work he had put in, not just on basketball, or sports, but on everything. And instead of some evaluation or score on some standardized test, here was a moment of clear-cut victory. This was the high you can't buy.

At some point in my celebration, I looked down at the rest of the crowd. They were staring up at me. For them this was just another rec league basketball game. They must have wondered what was wrong with me. The action on the court had stopped as the players and ref turned to see the crazy man in the stands. I sat down. The game proceeded and I could hear a murmur in the crowd as the word spread that it was our son's first basket. And little by little I heard other parents begin to cheer for our son. It was overwhelming. After years of feeling that no one else understood or cared what we were going through, for the first time, I heard them urging him on. The load had gotten lighter.

And I could feel my dad behind me, his hand on my shoulder, squeezing it, patting me on the back. He was there and he was as elated as we were. Some things are just too good, too powerful for even the separation of death to overcome.

I remained on a cloud as the game continued. Our son's teammates realized that those were his first points. And they started feeding him the ball. They were running the offense just for him. Maybe they just wanted to see me jump up and down again. Whatever the reason, a few minutes later, our son put up another shot and scored! And another! I cheered again, this time with a bit more self-control. The other parents cheered too.

After the game, which we won, we hugged our son and celebrated. I shook hands with all of his teammates and coach and wanted to hug them too. They had given me a gift beyond any price.

It is said that sports can be a metaphor for life. And surely more is made over mere games than should be. So many things go into winning and losing. The best team doesn't always win and the good guys don't always triumph. When I look back at our son's experience with sports I feel happy. For him, in the end, it was mostly about trying and not quitting, about being part of a team and practicing to become better. But for me, it was a gift he gave to me and my dad of a moment of victory that I will never forget.

****

A few years, later, in high school, we encouraged our son to go out for a sport. We had heard that the tennis team was a friendly group with a watchful, pleasant coach. They had also been pretty successful over the past few years and sent a couple of kids off to college on tennis scholarships. It was a non-contact sport and we felt that it was worth a try, so when our son agreed to give it a go, we were very happy. In the summer before his freshman year, we had sent him to "private" tennis lessons. He had shown some aptitude for the sport and even seemed to enjoy it.

Digression. - As much as we wanted to have both of our kids outside playing in the sunshine, the reality was that they preferred being inside, watching TV or videos or playing video games. I don't think this makes them at all unusual. But new friends, as we often explained to them both, are unlikely to simply show up at the door. You would have to go out and meet them. But there is a "comfort zone" to one's own room. And as much of a challenge socially and academically as school was, we did not begrudge them the sanctuary of their private time. So we had to push a little to get our son to go to tennis lessons and to stay after school for team practices and games. And push we did. - End of digression.

The tennis team had an "open registration". That is, everyone who signed up made the team. Our son was taller than most kids and had a long reach. He was developing the coordination needed to play. And he tried hard. He always tried hard. What more could a coach ask for? As a freshman, he played mostly doubles. Since there was a limited number of courts, underclass doubles players had to wait until the senior singles matches were over. The coach required the team members, when not actually playing, to cheer on their teammates. Our son spent hours cheering on his teammates. But it was a wonderful thing to hear them returning the favor, especially when he won!

The team had monthly spaghetti dinners following practice. We hoped these would continue the encouraging trend of acceptance of our son into the team. After one or two of these, an occasion came up when somehow, our son was the one team member who didn't get the word about where the dinner was to be held and didn't get a ride with anyone. It may have been a random thing, but it stung. And it was never explained to us how this had happened. No apology. Nothing. Although the coach was really big on team spirit and togetherness and support, he seemed to have developed a blind spot in this regard. I don't think our son went to another of those dinners in the two years that followed when he was on the team. He (and we) learned not to dwell on the negative.

Nonetheless, in the course of all the practices and the waiting around to play and the cheering on of teammates, our son, for the first time, was being accepted by a larger group without any labels or accommodations. He was simply one of the guys. We were always happy to see that, win or lose. It gave us hope that he and his peers were growing out of that insecure stage where everyone was quick to pick up on differences and pick on those who were different.

As freshman year gave way to sophomore year and then to junior year, we expected our son to gradually become a singles player who would not have to wait to play. Surely his turn had come, right? We never really found out why, but over those years it seemed the coach was changing the way he assigned the matches. He favored a very few players with the coveted early match spots and let players like our son and others, who had paid their dues over a couple of seasons, languish on the bench. A number of parents complained to the coach who simply dug his heels in and refused to change. At the end of his junior year, our son asked us if he could quit the team. By that time he was able to express to us why it wasn't fun for him anymore and that he preferred to use his time in video production after school, rather than waiting around for a chance to play, that might not ever come. In the face of his eloquence, we agreed.

I wonder what my son will remember about his times playing sports. I don't remember my own wins or losses as much as I remember my dad happily grabbing his mitt to have a catch with me or each of my grandfathers smiling with boyish glee as they threw me a ball. Maybe what sports teaches us isn't about winning and losing at all. Maybe sports just provides us with a little space to build the next part of the long bridge that links the generations.

7

Always Bring a Gun to a Knife-fight

USUALLY, I have no problem getting to sleep. But there are those nights when I lie in bed and bad thoughts come to me. They are often memories of those moments in my life when I said or did the wrong thing. I can hear the stupid thing I said echo over and over. I see the ugly thing I did in slow motion. I shudder and try to think of something else. But sometimes it's not so easy to turn the page or change the channel.

As our son's senior year of high school approached, we thought long and hard about what our next move would be. We consulted with, Dr. Williams, the expert who ran a center for children with special needs and one of our son's social groups. Dr. Williams talked about the need for a transition year. The transition year would continue the educational path he was on and would include living away from home in a supervised house with other high-functioning young men with autism spectrum disorders.

There were benefits to this approach. The educational classes would be at a local community college. Our son would be following a similar trajectory to the one that his neuro-typical peers would. Living away from home would afford him a new experience of dealing with people in close quarters and foster independence. The supervisors at the house would prevent him from self-isolating. There would be scheduled activities and duties. He would be responsible for shopping, some cooking and chores. It sounded like everything our son needed.

Dr. Williams recommended that our son not graduate from high school with his class. He could "walk" and participate in the graduation activities, but he would not receive his diploma. This kept the school system "on the hook" to manage and pay for the transition year. And the year-long live-away experience was not cheap. It cost more than a year at a top Ivy League college! But the school system was legally obligated to provide "an appropriate education" for every student who had a disability diagnosis through age 21. This was a little-known fact that the school system did not advertise. It reinforced that we had done the right thing by getting a diagnosis and undertaking the laborious PPT/IEP process all those years ago.

Through Dr. Williams, we participated in a support group with other parents from our son's social group. I recommend this to everyone. You will learn a lot about how the system works and even more about human nature. We heard heartbreaking stories about families who broke under the strain of life and dealing with special needs children. If having kids tease you at school is bad, what is it called when your father cuts off contact by throwing your belongings out onto the lawn and locking you out?

We heard how one school district, seeking to save the cost of continuing the education of one young man, called him in the day after he turned 18 and coerced him into signing away his rights to that continued education. This may be the definition of pure evil. Fortunately, we learned of a lawyer whose work had essentially defined the rights of special needs students in our state. He had helped establish the right of those students to a public school education to age 21. School districts quaked with fear at the mention of his name. And they hated to have the parents of special needs students in their district engage him. We contacted him immediately.

At the last PPT meeting of our son's junior year, we brought up the idea of the transition year with our son living in the residential transition academy. All of the teachers at the meeting thought it was a great idea. Our son was ready for the academic challenge of community college classes. His guidance counsellor agreed that he would thrive in a new living environment and that "going off to college" like so many of his peers would give him confidence and allow him to fit in more. The idea of "walking" with his class while not technically "graduating" was well-received.

Then it was the turn of the school district's financial watchdog, Mrs. Blake, to speak. She was an officious, unsmiling woman. She flatly said that the school district would not pay for the transition year. There was no discussion of the costs. It was a "no". The principal of the high school mumbled something about being able to cobble together a similar program using district resources. Surely, some compromise accommodation could be reached.

We left the meeting resolving to contact the lawyer and gird for the fight. We had been warned that this would happen. But we were shaking with anger and uncertainty about this most important choice for our son as we made our way to our car.

Outside, in the parking lot, we were greeted by a well-dressed man with a friendly smile. He introduced himself as

James Cooper, the consultant to the school district. He handled matters like the one we had just brought up to the PPT. We weren't looking for a fight in the parking lot, but we weren't afraid of it either. We explained our idea about a transition year and our son living at the transition academy. We told him how all of the district personnel who are involved in the education and guidance of our son thought it was a great idea and how Mrs. Blake had shut it down.

Mr. Cooper smiled and told us not to be discouraged. He told us how obvious it was that we were thoughtful, caring parents. He complimented us on devising such a wonderful plan for our son. He said it sounded like it was just what our son needed and that perhaps the district could be convinced to pay for most or all of the transition academy year.

As we drove home, we felt we had an ally who was well-positioned within the school district. Maybe all was not lost. Just to be on the safe side, we engaged the lawyer to help us if and when the discussion became a fight.

Mr. Cooper appeared at the first PPT meeting of our son's senior year. He recommended yet another comprehensive program of placement testing to confirm that our son was ready for a transition program such as we proposed. The school district paid for all of this testing. They held a "feel-good" meeting where all of our son's teacher and evaluators and experts gathered to say that our son was a high-performing student, how he had progressed and been mainstreamed and was primed for success. "The sky is the limit", one of them said to general agreement.

The minutes from this meeting and all the others, along with all the test results were forwarded to our attorney. He said that we had all the ammo we would need and assigned

Beth Wilson, sharp young attorney, to handle our case. The legal team was confident and ready even as it seemed that the school district was coming around to our idea of the transition academy year. Beth warned us to be ready for the rug to be pulled out from under our feet.

The school district waited until late in the year, days before graduation. The PPT gathered in a large office with a noisy window unit air conditioner. We all discussed what a fine year our son had academically. As had been the case every year, based on nothing measurable, they determined that all of his goals had been met and they had done a great job. They complimented us on being wonderful, involved parents. And then they grabbed the rug and gave it a mighty tug.

The PPT had reviewed our transition academy year plan. We had provided an hourly breakdown of what our son would be doing each day of each week. We had provided letters from the academy saying that he was an ideal candidate for placement. We had provided letters from Dr. Williams saying that this was the best option on the table. It was time for them to say yes or no. All of our son's teachers bowed their heads as if they were ashamed of what was about to happen.

The once smiling Mr. Cooper said that it was the opinion of the school district that our transition academy year plan was "not appropriate" for our son. This was not about money, he said. It was about the plan (that he had seen as marvelous one year earlier in the parking lot) not being "appropriate". He kept using the word "appropriate" because the law required the district to do what was "appropriate". He was building the district's case against us. The fight was on.

There followed a settlement process and agreement with the district which we agreed would remain confidential. But any parents who find themselves in a similar situation should be sure to know their rights, retain competent legal counsel experienced in such matters, fight hard for their kids and get everything you can get for them.

A week later we watched our son graduate with all the other seniors, right on time. We flashed back to nursery school and elementary school and middle school and all the meetings and all the testing and, as I snapped the picture of him receiving his diploma, I cried tears of joy and relief. He looked at me, beaming. He was special alright. He was the finest kid at that ceremony. He had persevered and triumphed. And we had been with him every step of the way. It was a perfect moment of family joy and victory.

And when I have trouble getting to sleep some nights, I can recall our beautiful son, in his blue cap and gown, the yellow tassel swaying, smiling a perfect smile at me as he grasped his high school diploma. And I drift off to sleep with a smile on my face too.

I know that Mrs. Blake and Mr. Cooper were only doing their jobs. But they knew as well I did that they were working against a wonderful young man who had worked like hell to overcome so much. And yet they did their jobs trying to place one more obstacle in his way. I wonder how they sleep.

8

IF AT FIRST YOU DON'T SUCCEED

WE'VE all seen those lucky few individuals who seem to walk through life without ever tasting hardship or failure. I think of the pro athletes who were always the first kid picked for every team. They were always the best player, no matter what the game. They won at every level. They made the all-star team, the traveling team, the varsity, first string team. They were recruited by colleges who handed them full-ride scholarships. They graduated without attending a single class and were drafted by the pros. They dated the cheerleaders, then models, then actresses. They made it into the Hall of Fame and retired to sell luxury cars.

It must be nice. For most of us, though, life involves struggle. And sometimes failure. But the irony is, you learn more from failing and trying again than from succeeding the first time.

Special education is a wonderful thing. Those dedicated teachers who find innovative ways to convey lessons to students who don't learn the same way most student do are a godsend. But the special ed students deserve praise too. Struggling without quitting to learn what many take for granted is a big mountain to climb.

Driving is one of those skills that most of us take for granted. At age 16, we study the driver's manual and spend a few weeks with mom or dad or an instructor learning to gauge turns and braking distances, to parallel park and make three-point turns. For most of us, it's not such a challenge.

But that written test can be a challenge for a student who has trouble with written verbal comprehension. Even a student who understands the rules of the road can struggle with multiple-choice questions that offer nuanced shades of difference between the correct answer and the others. Add to this the anxiety of taking any formal written test. And change the venue from a quiet classroom to the noisy DMV office. And add in the high stakes of getting a license or not getting one. Oh, and did I mention that lots of your peers will be there at the same time? They'll want to know how you did.

Our son took to driving very naturally. He had observed my wife and me driving for years and had a great understanding of how the car worked and what safe driving entailed. My wife did the road work with him and reported that he was careful, safe and attentive. He mastered all aspects of driving quickly. To this day, he is the safest driver I have ever ridden with. He comes to a complete stop at stop signs, signals for every turn and obeys every rule without exception. His natural friendliness translates to courtesy behind the wheel. He was quickly ready for his driver's road test.

Then there was the written test. He studied the driver's manual. He and I went over all of the sections. So much of it was devoted to the process of getting a license and the consequences of drinking and driving. He dutifully learned all of the penalties and processes. He knew how to get a license, why one might lose his license and how to get it back if you did lose it.

There were three or four "sample test questions". He quickly memorized those. Then the day came for him to take his test.

I was at work. It was a cloudy afternoon. I wasn't particularly busy and had time to think about what time he might get to the DMV, how he might do, and to worry. The phone rang around 3pm. My wife told me he had come within one question of passing. One lousy question. I asked how he was taking it. He was crushed.

In special ed classes they are able to lower the bar, to evaluate without the cold black and white of pass versus fail. Even though our son had displayed his academic weaknesses (as well as his strengths), failure hadn't often been a cold slap in the face the way this was. One lousy question.

I went outside to walk around the block. I wanted to cry. A cold breeze blew in my face and it began to drizzle. As I walked, I resolved to do everything I could to help our son clear this hurdle. He had already come so far. His reading and writing were progressing to grade level. He was a math whiz. He could do this. After all, he had come within one lousy question of passing.

At home, he didn't want to talk about it. My wife told me that the "written" test was actually administered on a computer touchscreen. There were subtle rules. You could skip a question and go back to it later. It wasn't clear to us if he had gone back to the ones he skipped. Maybe that was where he lost points. It was hard to get him to tell me about the questions he missed. Again, it wasn't clear. It sounded like the computer would indicate a wrong answer as soon as he made the choice, adding to the pressure.

My wife and I dug in. There had to be a way. She called DMV and found out that a true written test, on a piece of paper, could be given to any student who requested one, but only at the DMV office a few towns over. Great! There wouldn't be any kids from our son's school there.

And I looked online and found some more practice test questions. I put together a 20 question test, just like the one the DMV gave. After a few days, our son had gotten over his disappointment and we began to study again. We went over every page in the manual and he answered all 20 practice questions perfectly.

A week later he was at a different DMV office taking a written test on paper. He missed passing by a two questions. He was crushed again.

After a few days, I carefully questioned him about the experience. It seemed that the questions he missed had been similar to the ones we had studied, but the wording had been changed. They were trick questions! They weren't asking when you DID have the right of way, they were asking when you DIDN'T have the right of way. They had zeroed in to the very crux of the reading disability our son had.

Some things should not be graded on a curve. Driving is one of them. But the wording on the test had nothing to do with knowledge of the rules, it was a test of reading comprehension at a pretty high level. This might be too much. The more I thought about how unfair this was, the madder I became. There was only one thing to do. My son would have to learn to recognize the most detailed, nuanced variations in the way that each question could be asked and be able to pick the one that was correct, or incorrect, depending on what was being asked for.

The next practice test I presented him with had 50 questions. Many of them simply twisted the verbiage of questions he already knew the answers to. A week of drilling and he was ready for the DMV a third time. This time he missed by one question again. So close. But he was ready to quit. I wanted to exhort him to bear down, but my wife told me to back off. She's so smart.

A few days later, he came to me. He told me about the questions he had missed. I looked at my practice test. I saw another way the questions could be twisted and negated to yield a different answer. The new practice test I made had 100 questions. Some questions were asked five different ways. After two weeks, he headed to the DMV for his fourth shot. He missed by two questions.

Doubt and despair are insidious forces. They come to us at our weakest moments. They indulge our desire to give up and to lay down and let the world move on without us. They confirm our darkest fears about ourselves. They are monsters we let grow large in the recesses of our minds. And there is only one way to beat them.

We waited a week before we resumed our work. As we reviewed I could see that he had not only mastered the material about driving and the law and getting a license, but he was becoming adept at recognizing the ways a question could be phrased and how subtle changes in wording could make one answer right and the others wrong. He had mastered the "all of the above", the "none of the above", the "both A and C" and the "Neither B nor D" questions.

I saw our son steel himself to the task. He would not allow

himself to be optimistic, but he wouldn't quit either. He kept asking me for more questions. The practice test now had over 200 questions, ten times the number on the DMV test. And he consistently answered them all correctly. He and my wife would be at the DMV the following afternoon. Fifth try.

I was at work trying not to think about it, but thinking of nothing else. I felt my cellphone vibrate and took a deep breath. The text message read, "Passed." I wanted to explode, but I knew that there were two parts to the driver's test. The written test and the road test.

"Passed both?" I replied.

"Y", was all the next message said. And I was elated. I hugged everyone I saw at work. I fought back tears of joy unsuccessfully. Back at home, I hugged him and my wife. We called our daughter, my mother, my in-laws and everyone else we could think of. Our son seemed overwhelmed by our reaction. He had a big smile, but was modest by instinct. Life had taught him that the next challenge was never far away and it didn't pay to get cocky. But I wanted him to know that such clear victories, after hard-fought campaigns are worth celebrating. Joy is something to be savored. If you are going to feel the sting of the blow, then you have to revel in the triumph of the accomplishment.

As we hugged and danced and jumped for joy that night, I considered how those fortunate few who never fail at anything could never know we what we were feeling right then. I wondered if they fear defeat as a shadowy, unknown menace. They will never know the true measure of their own courage. And I feel sorry for them. I truly do. Maybe the greatest victory is the knowledge that you got up one time more than you got knocked down.

9

Bullies - Big and Small and a Sign

THERE are two stories I always think of when I hear the word "bully". The first is the Biblical story of David and Goliath as I was taught it when I was a child. David, the meek and mild shepherd boy, steps out onto the field of battle against the Philistine's champion warrior, the giant, Goliath. Against all odds, the shepherd boy fells the frightful foe with one well slung stone.

The other is a story that I read in second grade. It was called, "The Bully of Barkham Street" by Mary Stolz. It was the sequel to "A Dog on Barkham Street". Marty Hastings is introduced in the first book as an evil bully who does all he can to make the hero, Edward, and his dog, Argess, miserable. We never question why Marty is so evil. He simply serves the dramatic purpose of being the bad guy over whom Edward and Argess eventually triumph. But in the sequel, we find out what made Marty become so mean and we learn that life isn't always as simple as bad guys and good guys. I recommend both books for kids.

Bullies are the reminder that life is not always fair or safe.

They force us to grow up, get tough, and to put away the innocence of childhood, sometimes forever. Bullies force us to consider violence. How can we protect ourselves from it? And can we inflict it on another in order to protect ourselves? Bullies force us to define ourselves in real terms. We must balance the willingness to enter into righteous combat as David did with the compassion to understand the Marty Hastings of the world and the factors that put them on the path to conflict with us.

We lived in a rural-suburban neighborhood. There were quite a few boys our son's age. Things had changed in the years since my wife and I were kids. This neighborhood was a bit more spread out than the track housing we grew up in. Yes, there were kids out playing, but it seemed to be more cliquish and less come-one, come-all. This was a time when mothers arranged "playdates" for kids. These meetings of mothers and kids at parks or playgrounds gave the kids a chance to run around and the mothers a chance to exchange gossip and chat.

It was a month or two after our son had been in the town's popular nursery school. We had taken him out because he wasn't happy there. The nice ladies who ran it didn't know quite how to deal with a non-communicative child who didn't want to stop doing one activity he was happy with to start another that he didn't enjoy as much. There was no major incident. We could just tell that this was not the place for our son at that time.

My wife arranged a playdate for our son with several of the neighborhood boys his age at our house. It went well. The three boys played nicely together, although our son eventually settled into some parallel play beside, but not really with, the other two boys. The next day my wife was chatting with the mother of one of the boys and asked when the next playdate might be.

Her response immediate, as if she had been thinking about it and had her answer prepared.

"There won't be any more playdates," she said coldly.

She offered no explanation and no apology. Our sons would grow up down the street from each other but not as friends or playmates. This was a very harsh reality. There would be a few adults who would actively shun us and our son because of his differences. Many more had love and compassion in their hearts and got to see the miracle that he became.

A few years later, in first grade, the Japanese cartoon series *Pokemon* was very popular. Our son was a huge fan and, like many other kids his age, collected the cards that had different characters from the show on them. I helped him put together a notebook with his collection in it, just like the notebooks I had for my baseball cards. He would page through that notebook endlessly, lecturing me about the characters and their powers.

One day I got a call at work from my wife. She was upset. Our son had come home from school frantic because his *Pokemon* collection had been decimated. It took a while to get the facts straight, but it turned out that some older kids had spied him on the playground with his beloved notebook and done some "trading" with him. The result was all of his favorite cards were gone. Worse yet, these were neighborhood kids who had previously shunned our son who were now victimizing him in this cruel way.

I left work in a righteous fury. I sped home and tried to make sense of how anyone could swindle a sweet kid out of his prized possessions. I kicked myself for allowing him to take the notebook to school. We had naively thought it would give him some common ground with his peers and might facilitate making a friend. I was apoplectic. My wife talked me down. If I couldn't get justice from third graders, I could at least repair the damage they had done. I sped to a card shop and bought every *Pokemon* card they had. I rushed home and together we rebuilt our son's collection. He ended up losing a few old favorites, but getting a few new ones. And we had learned a lesson. School is not a safe haven.

Over the next four years, this lesson would be hammered home.

My wife volunteered in our son's classroom from kindergarten on as a classroom aide and to watch over him. Inevitably, the issues would arise when she was not there. Early on, our son was not aware of what may have been going on. Verbal taunting and teasing may have gone unnoticed. But eventually, he came to understand that a certain boy, let's call him Marty, was directing negative attention toward him. Our son was a very strong child. Once he had been exposed to this form of abuse a time or two, he steeled himself to it. He did not want to draw further attention to himself. He was becoming conscious of how he was viewed by others.

And Marty became a smart bully. He learned to wait until the teacher was looking the other way or stepped out of the classroom. Then he would unleash the teasing and name-calling. I was not there to see or hear it. Nor was my wife. And so I can't say exactly how it was or how bad it got. But other kids saw it. And like a cancer, it spread. It became known that you could pick on our son and nothing would happen to you. For some young boys, seeking to boost their standing in the pecking order, it was the thing to do.

I was at one of our son's soccer games one Saturday. As I stood along the sidelines, I heard two boys talking behind me.

One said, "See that kid?" He indicated our son. "It's easy to make him cry."

I spun around and glared at that little boy. I wish I could tell you that I said something wise to him or that I had some snappy quip to shut him up. A part of me wanted to threaten him and scare him to the point of tears. But I had no such words. I just stared at him. He stopped talking and looked up at me. I don't know if he knew I was "that kid's" dad or not. But he had a sick, guilty look on his face. He and his pal walked away. And as I turned and looked back at the soccer field and saw our son running, trying so hard to do his best, I understood a bit better the mountain he had to climb each day and the obstacles that life had put in his path.

My wife took more effective action than I did with my withering glare. Through her work in the classroom, she compiled a list of the kids who were kind to our son, as well as the bullies and those who were not so kind. At meetings with the teachers and school officials, she was able to engineer class assignments and seating arrangements to surround our son with the kinder kids. We had to educate the teachers about the kids in their own classes. It was strange to us that they often could not see which ones were the troublemakers. Each year we would learn more about how to protect our son. We would make sure he was seated near the front of the room, close to the teacher. We would make sure his tormenters were as far from him as possible. Sometimes we were able to arrange for them to be in a different class altogether. But not always. You see, the troublemakers were troubled themselves. They often had issues that the teachers could not discuss with us that required them to be in the class with our son. (Shades of Marty Hastings!) I found it hard to have compassion for a child who made a hobby of bullying my son. But through her presence in the classroom, through intervening in things like seating, my wife was able to protect him somewhat. And every year, by the end of the year, we would have fine-tuned his school day experience to a point where our son had the best learning environment possible.

Then would come the next year and we had to start all over. Just as we had with academic issues, we would have to intervene on these issues too. From square one. First, we would have to educate the teacher about who our son was. He was such a compliant child and so adept at blending in, he would usually fool the teacher into thinking he had very few issues. They would look at my wife and me as overly-involved, overprotective parents. Then there would be an incident, usually pretty minor, and the teacher would come back to us and actually listen. Even in the formal Planning and Placement Team (PPT) meetings, we would have to start over again and again when the school psychologist, or principal or social worker would go on leave or be replaced or quit. We would have to retrain another member or group. We got to be pretty good at it be the end of elementary school. But there were so many frustrations.

We would think we had set up a good system to protect our son, and then we would learn of a flaw in the system. Yes, we had gotten him with the "better" fourth grade teacher who had a "special education background". And yes, Marty was in the other fourth grade class, but guess what? Both classes take music at the same time in the same space with a teacher who had not been informed about any of the students' special needs. And who ended up right next to our son? Marty! And so our son went from enjoying music to hating it. And it was up to us to do the detective work to figure out why. The music teacher was clueless and Marty had become skilled at poking our son so that she only saw his retaliation and not Marty's provocation. Neat, huh?

And once we got music sorted out, and our son had quit the choir (Thanks, Marty!), the situation moved to art! The art teacher was just as clueless as the music teacher had been and who sat across from our son? Marty! And here he was armed with paint to sling and clay to throw and he could deface whatever work our son managed to create. Charming. And so we had to intervene again and educate yet another educator about special needs students and how some kids needed actual supervision.

But the saddest of these episodes involved gym. I actually knew and liked the male gym teacher. He was a great guy. He showed an interest in our son and often asked about him and his sister who had been his student three years before. I never highlighted our son's differences when I discussed him in this way. The gym teacher was always complimentary about his effort, ability and sweet personality. These were things no teacher could miss. And so it was a double shock when we came to find out that there were problems in gym class with Marty, teasing and physically interfering with our son! And it became known to the teacher and yet it continued! Once again we found ourselves in a PPT stunned that all of the school staff who had charge of the students at one time or another had not been made aware of the special needs of the students! This time it was my friend, the gym teacher! The next time I saw him, he came up to me almost in tears. He told me that he had no idea about our son's diagnosis. And when he saw Marty bullying him, he set about to try to make them friends. He made them shake hands and partner up again and again. Marty must have been in his glory. His victim was being served to him on a plate! As soon as the teacher became aware of the truth, he separated the two and made sure that they were never on the same playing field or locker room at the same time. He apologized profusely and told me that he coached special Olympians and was trained to deal with such situations, but had never been given any indication from the administration that there was any special needs situation.

Marty became less and less of a factor in our son's life after elementary school as Marty's own issues got worse and his obvious anti-social behavior was red-flagged. The last we heard he was in counseling and receiving a number of therapies.

Outside of the classroom, school still offered opportunities for bullies to prey on our son. The school bus was a haven for the little monsters. As luck would have it, although it is only a ten minute drive to the school, the route the bus took made the ride closer to an hour. The bullying didn't begin on day one, and it was difficult for us to get an accurate picture of the extent of it. There was apparently a steady build-up of name-calling and antagonism by a group of kids who lived a half dozen doors down from us who became bolder as their bad behavior went unchecked.

How do you tell your neighbor that their little darling child is systematically victimizing a special needs student? How do you get someone to understand that the tough "love" they give to their own kids is getting passed on as bullying to your child? And who is there to protect the victimized children on the bus from the bullies? The driver? I don't wish to offend the legions of wonderful people who safely drive school buses at ungodly hours in all kinds of weather, but few of them are trained to deal with bullying, much less protection of special need students, while driving a bus!

However, this was one arena where we got an effective response from the school administration. You see, school bus ridership is a privilege, not a right. And misbehavior on a school bus was taken very seriously, as it should be, by our school district. Once we identified the school bus bullies and got their names to the principal, the bullies' parents were notified that their little darlings would have to be driven to school every morning. Since both parents in these households worked, this meant that someone would be late for work every day! It's maybe just too bad if you happen to raise a nasty kid who bullies special needs students. But it's a crisis if your precious one starts affecting your job (and potentially your income)! Apparently, the bus bullies were sufficiently disciplined by their parents that there was never another peep from them. And my wife was often able to drive our son to school.

Away from school, bullies were fewer and further between, but they were there. Our church operates a wonderful sleep-away camp in the woods of upstate Connecticut. There are supervised activities, games, swimming in a pristine lake and fellowship with other youth. The housing is in bunkhouses with a chaperoning teen looking after the younger kids. We carefully looked into how well-suited the arrangements were to a kid like our son and sent him off for the week. The supervisors and chaperones were informed, to some extent about his differences. It is always difficult to know how and how much to communicate such information in such situations. Few adult experts are trained to properly deal with special needs kids, let alone volunteering teens.

My wife visited him a couple of times during the week to

check on him. He was doing pretty well, getting along with, if not befriending the other kids. But he had acquired a personal tormentor named Nick. It was always difficult to get particular details. Our son could not express himself well enough to tell us in detail, in proper sequence, what was being done, but we got enough information to know that Nick was calling him names, throwing rocks at him and generally making his week miserable, all carefully out of sight of the supervisors and chaperones.

When the day came to pick our son up at the end of the week, he was beyond happy to see us. He hugged us like he would never let go. And God bless my wife. She sought out Nick, the boy who had made such a project of harassing him for the week. I was there when she found him. She let him have it with both barrels.

"Nick, my son tells me that you called him names and teased him all week. He told me that you threw rocks at him while you were swimming. He told me you said nasty things about him to the other kids. Why did you do that? How would you feel if someone did that to you? What if someone made fun of your differences? Would you like that?"

Nick could not look up at her. His shield of anonymity had been stripped away. Maybe for the first time he began to see that our son wasn't just a target for his amusement, but a person like he was. He looked like he might cry.

"Do you have something to say? Do you want to say you are sorry?"

Nick mumbled an apology without looking up. He couldn't meet our son's eye. Then he asked my wife if she was going to tell his parents.

"Oh yes! Of course. Don't you think your parents should know what you have done?"

Now he started to sob. In my righteous anger I hoped he was learning a lesson he would never forget. I hoped that his parents would be appalled and would never let him forget. I walked with our son back to our car. He had moved on and was eager to get back to his comfort zone. He had enjoyed the swimming and the food and some of the other activities. He didn't dwell on the negative. Thank goodness he rarely has. My wife found Nick's parents and then joined us in the car.

My hopes of satisfaction were dashed. Rather than being furious and promising to teach their little monster a lesson, they were sad and disappointed. As is so often the case, Nick had his own issues. He had trouble making friends. He had learning issues. I tried to have compassion for him, but my desire to protect our son and my anger on his behalf wouldn't let me fully do so. But I couldn't be as angry and demonize Nick the way I had wanted to either. Good guys and bad guys were easier spot when David fought Goliath.

A Sign

Of course, not every child is a bully. Most are benign. Few will stand up for a bullied kid, but most are simply trying to get through their own lives as best they can. And every so often you meet a child who opens your eyes.

Our family took a cruise one winter vacation when our son was about five years old, shortly after we had come to grips with his diagnosis. Our kids loved running all over the grand ship, eating pizza all day long and swimming in the pool. As is often the case on board a ship, there are large tables and randomly assigned dinner companions. Although our son was never any trouble and didn't attract attention through misbehavior, it could be awkward when friendly strangers would try to make conversation and he would not respond or he would echo their words back at them. We nervously approached our dinner companions for the evening. That night we dined in a special themed restaurant. The walls were decorated with fairy-tale characters drawn in black and white.

We introduced ourselves to the Yates family! Yes, they had the same last name as we did! Remarkable. The husband and wife were charming people from Massachusetts. They had a younger son about the age of our daughter. And they had a seventeen year old son who had several severe afflictions including autism. My wife and Mrs. Yates spoke extensively throughout the meal. We learned of the struggles they had had in trying to get services for their son. They had, in fact, pioneered a number of initiatives within the Massachusetts legal system on his behalf. They had courage beyond words and had been indefatigable in their efforts. In spite of his lack of verbal ability, he was making progress and would be receiving services and education through a university soon. We were amazed.

As I sat, at first uncomfortably, next to the Yates' son, I began to see past his disabilities. He would smile and laugh without reservation. He was wholly unselfconscious. And when he expressed himself, he had something to say. He was a person with interesting thoughts and feelings. I began to see how small and unimportant his terrible afflictions really were to him and his family. Who he was was so much more important than who he wasn't. What he could do was so much more vital than what he couldn't do. I felt very small sitting next to this shining, remarkable soul. Here was a person who was overcoming a mountain of challenges through his own Herculean efforts, the love of his family and the grace of God. I looked at our son and knew with absolute certainty, probably for the very first time, that he could do the same. And the name of the amazing young man who first made me feel real hope? Steven Yates. I cried that night out of gratitude for having met this young man who shared my name. I hope he reads this and knows how much he helped me, through the powerful and life-changing example of his life. Thank you, Steven Yates.

As our meal progressed, the black and white fairy-tale characters on the walls slowly changed into color. The quiet, barely audible music swelled into the familiar, happy tunes of beloved childhood favorite movies. And just like all those wonderful old movies, I came to see that our lives, most especially our son's life, might just have its own "happily ever after".

10

SOCIAL GROUPS AND THE TRANSITION ACADEMY

ONE of the things that is most challenging about trying to help someone learn how to socialize with others is that it seems to be such a non-specific skill. In every social group setting, people assume different roles. Maybe one person drives the conversation. Another person may be playfully joking with everyone. Still another may be quietly listening and only contribute carefully chosen words sparingly. How are those skills taught?

As with most things, the answer turns out to be practice and trial and error. In an effort to provide a safe arena for such social practice for students who need it, schools often offer lunchtime "social groups" with such clever names as "lunch bunch" or "super friends". There is usually a teacher assigned to monitor and supervise these meetings. As with all such activities, it is difficult to determine their effectiveness.

At school, lunch time and recess are important times for social interaction. And while some students are not equipped to successfully engage in these interactions, these "lunch bunches" pull them out of the arena altogether. And although I have not attended these sessions, I suspect that, based on what I was able to learn from our son, they generally end up centered around simple games and other activities that are not building the kind of spontaneous conversational and relational skills that neurotypical students have and take for granted.

How, then, can such skills be taught? We were fortunate enough to find Dr. Williams, a skilled child psychologist who ran a private center for children with special needs, when our son was in his early teens. Dr. Williams ran a number of social groups after school hours, usually in the evenings in a large, comfortable room located across from his office. The room had comfortable chairs and big-screen TV. The group our son attended had about a dozen young men who would gather weekly for 90 minutes. Dr. Williams would guide them through discussions where each was encouraged to offer some contribution. The topics were directly related to the mechanics of starting and carrying on conversations, how to act when emergencies occur, what constitutes appropriate conversation in various contexts and other "nuts and bolts" subjects that the young men needed to learn.

Dr. Williams would describe a scenario and try to elicit comments from the students about how they would react and what they might say. Sometimes there were videos showing such scenes acted out that the students could comment on. In addition to learning the mechanics of social interaction, the students built relationships with each other. For many of them, these were the first friendships they had ever had. They could see how each of them was different and how each was similar. As they would go around the circle taking turns making their comments, sometimes one would be unable to add anything. They would encourage each other and offer support. They would often share stories from their own lives of successes or failures they had experienced in the previous week.

Dr. Williams was able to promote proper social skills and appropriate conversation through practice even as he was building some real social relationships. All of this took part away from the school environment.

Our son would tell us about the other young men and what they had to say in the group sessions as well as what he would say. Sometimes we would suggest things he might bring up and other times he would report that he shared interests with one of the other guys and that they talked about that. Once he got his driver's license, he would drive himself to the Thursday night meetings and that was a source of admiration and awe to the other young men. Again, we realized how fortunate he was as many of these young men might never achieve that freedom.

Dr. Williams was able to offer the families of these young men feedback that they were not getting from the schools. He could also offer other resources that might be available across the state or region. And he had credentials that allowed him to participate in school PPT meetings.

Such assistance is not free, nor is it cheap. We found few such effective programs that offered this kind of expert knowledge being brought to bear in a hands-on way to systematically educate young people on the autism spectrum in this way. And so it was more than worth the cost.

Through Dr. Williams, we found a vocational-education program that offered a similar well-supervised, credentialed environment for social skills training that had a different setting. This facility was a house in a residential neighborhood. A group of young men and women of high school age met there weekly after school and had supervised, guided social experiences as well as some free time to practice what they had learned. Having a home-like setting with a spacious backyard for cookouts and game-playing put the social skills training in a more realistic context.

In addition to staff that were often college students working toward degrees in special ed, the voc-ed facility had some "model" members who provided examples of proper social interactions and offered real friendship in a controlled, safe environment.

These kinds of facilities were very beneficial to our son. I urge parents to seek out such resources through local autism support groups, state disability offices, school systems and private educational counsellors. There are even special education programs at the college level. Given the apparent increase in the number of diagnosed autism spectrum cases, the number of such resources may be expected to grow over time. But, again, these programs are generally quite expensive.

****

Following graduation from high school, we felt that our son was ready for a different experience that would take him out of his comfort zone and challenge him to stand on his own. The voc-ed organization that had hosted the after school social group offered a unique "transition academy" program.

They owned a house in a nice residential neighborhood that could accommodate 6-8 young men on a live-in basis. The house was close to a local community college and offered van service to and from classes. There were local businesses that had partnered with them to offer jobs to some of the residents.

In the house, the resident students would be supervised by one live-in counsellor and a staff of aides and counsellors who were present during the day to offer practical instruction in life skills like cooking and laundry and to assist with signing up for classes and filling out employment applications. The resident students were responsible for shopping for their own food and personal items, cooking one meal a week, cleaning their rooms and maintaining the living space.

Most of the resident students had roommates and "alone time" was minimized while social interaction was nearly unavoidable. It was truly a transition from living at home with mom and dad to a dorm-like, more independent way of life.

Our son had a roommate who he had met at Dr. William's social group. After half a year, that young man moved out and our son had a single room to himself. It was good experience for him to deal with people who did not always agree with him and who were different from him in many ways. He loved the courses at the community college and spent his spare time on the campus. He learned to cook a few dishes and to do his laundry. He also learned the joy of coming home to a quiet, clean house to visit mom and dad on the holidays!

After the transition year was over, our son moved back in with us and currently attends community college pursuing a couple of certificates in the field of audio and video production. Given the success he has enjoyed to date, he may choose to pursue a degree in communication, or seek employment in the next few years.

As much as I have criticized the public school system, I must admit that none of the private social groups or even the transition academy were perfect either. But they offered the best options we could find at the time to give our son the best opportunity to grow, to learn and to succeed, with the goal of living a happy, productive, independent life. Our son has been the greatest of blessings in our lives. His journey thus far has been in turns, difficult, rewarding, frustrating, enriching, maddening and enlightening. We have seen a quiet little boy who was largely locked inside himself grow into a fine young man who has life goals within his reach and unlimited potential to go beyond his (and our) wildest dreams. It has given my life so much meaning and so much satisfaction. I cannot wait to see where it will go from here because the miracle continues.

Final Thoughts

WATCHING our son through these years has been the most incredible experience of my life. I was caught completely off guard by his journey through autism. I denied that it was happening, then feared the reality of it, slowly got on board with my wise and wonderful wife's efforts to understand and combat it and finally, almost too late, did what I could to help him emerge victorious.

As I write these final words, he is twenty years old. If you met him, you would see a tall, slim, handsome young man who is quiet at first, but warms quickly to friendly contact. He loves to laugh, to play music on his guitar, to create videos and to share his creations with the world. He is in many ways typical. He loves heavy metal music and video games. He is in many ways extraordinary. He has patience and tolerance and love in almost unlimited supply. He is everything a parent could want in a son.

It's impossible to know exactly what the future holds for him. But I am excited to find out. I believe that he will find his niche and make his mark in a creative way. I hope that his unique talents are fully realized and take him to amazing places he never dreamed of going. I pray that he finds a special someone, like I did, to share his life with, to grow with, and with whom to start a family that will have its own remarkable story.

I thank God for letting me be a part of his life.

****

As I said, this book should not be taken as legal or medical advice. We sought both in the course of our journey. Anyone who is trying to help a child with special needs should seek their own. Knowing the medical facts and your legal rights are of paramount importance. Get this information independently and seek second opinions.

In the time it took us to get from our first notions about autism to now, there has been much progress made in diagnosis, treatment and education. Please seek out the latest and best information. I hope you find great teachers, therapists and advisors. They are out there. There are few moments more rewarding than when you find a gifted expert who understands your situation and can offer you positive choices to move forward.

If you try something that does not appear to work, don't be discouraged. You don't have time for that.

Don't be afraid, as I was. I feared the labels that are mere words. I feared what people would think. I feared that I would make mistakes in trying to help. And my fear didn't help our son. It was only when I let my love for him overcome my fear that I was able to make my contribution to his miracle.

Embrace others who are on similar journeys of their own. You can gain strength by sharing your thoughts and by listening to stories of others. Don't waste precious time being shy or ashamed.

Most of all, take time to appreciate the person your child is every day. He or she is not a patient or a student or an experiment or a project or even a work in progress. He or she is a wonderful person and each day with them is a gift. Look hard enough and you will see the miracle that is always there.

www.ingramcontent.com/pod-product-compliance
Lightning Source LLC
Chambersburg PA
CBHW071407290426
44108CB00014B/1722